Anonymous

Ancient and Modern Scottish Songs, Heroic Ballads

Collected from memory, tradition, and ancient authors. The second edition. In two

volumes.

Anonymous

Ancient and Modern Scottish Songs, Heroic Ballads
Collected from memory, tradition, and ancient authors. The second edition. In two volumes.

ISBN/EAN: 9783744794206

Printed in Europe, USA, Canada, Australia, Japan

Cover: Foto ©Thomas Meinert / pixelio.de

More available books at **www.hansebooks.com**

ANCIENT AND MODERN

SCOTTISH SONGS,

HEROIC BALLADS,

ETC.

IN TWO VOLUMES.

VOLUME the SECOND.

The garb our Muses wore in former years.

HAMILTON.

EDINBURGH:

Printed by JOHN WOTHERSPOON,

FOR

JAMES DICKSON and CHARLES ELLIOT.

MDCCLXXVI.

ANCIENT AND MODERN .

SCOTTISH SONGS,

HEROIC BALLADS,

ETC.

COLLECTED FROM

MEMORY, TRADITION,

and

ANCIENT AUTHORS.

THE SECOND EDITION.

IN TWO VOLUMES.

VOLUME the SECOND.

EDINBURGH:

Printed by JOHN WOTHERSPOON,
FOR
JAMES DICKSON and CHARLES ELLIOT.
MDCCLXXVI.

FRAGMENTS

OF

SENTIMENTAL

AND

LOVE SONGS.

To its own Tune.

HOW can I be blyth or glad,
    Or in my mind contented be,
    When the bonny bonny lad that I loed beſt,
Is baniſh'd from my company.

Though he is baniſh'd for my ſake,
    I his true love will ſtill remain;
But O that I was, and I wiſh I was
    In the chamber where my true love is in.

I dare nae come to my true love,
    I dare nae either ſport or play,
For their evil evil tongues are going ſo gell,
    That I muſt kiſs and go my way.

Kiſſing is but a fooliſh fancy,
    It brings two lovers into ſin;
But O that I was, and I wiſh I was
    In the chamber where my love is in.

My true love is ftraight and tall,
  I had nae will to fay him nae,
For with his falfe, but fweet deluding tongue,
  He ftole my very heart away.

The Lowlands of Holland.

MY love has built a bonny fhip, and fet her on the fea,
With feven fcore good mariners to bear her company;
There's three fcore is funk, and threefcore dead at fea,
And the lowlands of Holland has twin'd my love and me.

My love he built another fhip, and fet her on the main,
And nane but twenty mariners for to bring her hame,
But the weary wind began to rife, and the fea began to rout,
My love then and his bonny fhip turn'd witherfhins about.

There fhall neither coif come on my head, nor comb come
    in my hair;
There fhall neither coal nor candle light fhine in my
    bower mair,
Nor will I love another one, until the day I die,
For I never lov'd a love but one, and he's drown'd in
    the fea.

O had your tongue my daughter dear, be ftill and be
    content,
There are mair lads in Galloway, ye need nae fair lament;
O! there is nane in Galloway, there's nane at a' for me,
For I never lov'd a love but ane, and he's drown'd in
    the fea.

LIZAE BAILLIE.

LIZAE BAILLIE's to Gartartan gane,
 To fee her fifter JEAN;
And there fhe's met wi' DUNCAN GRÆME,
 And he's convoy'd her haime.

" My bonny LIZAE BAILLIE,
 I'll row ye in my plaidie,
And ye maun gang alang wi' me,
 And be a Highland lady."

" I am fure they wad nae ca' me wife,
 Gin I wad gang wi' you, Sir;
For I can neither card nor fpin,
 Nor yet milk ewe or cow, Sir."

" My bonny LIZAE BAILLIE,
 Let nane o' thefe things daunt ye;
Ye'll hae nae need to card or fpin,
 Your mither weel can want ye."

Now fhe's caft aff her bonny fhoen,
 Made o' the gilded leather,
And fhe's put on her highland brogues,
 To fkip amang the heather:

And fhe's caft aff her bonny gown,
 Made o' the filk and fattin,
And fhe's put on a tartan plaid,
 To row amang the braken.

She wad nae hae a Lawland laird,
 Nor be an Englifh lady;
But fhe wad gang wi' DUNCAN GRÆME,
 And row her in his plaidie.

She was nae ten miles frae the town,
    When she began to weary ;
She aften looked back, and said,
    " Farewell to Caftlecarry.

" The firft place I faw my DUNCAN GRÆME
    Was near yon holland bush.
My father took frae me my rings,
    My rings but and my purfe,

" But I wad nae gie my DUNCAN GRÆME
    For a' my father's land,
Though it were ten times ten times mair,
    And a' at my command."

                *   *   *   *

Now wae be to you, loggerheads,
    That dwell near Caftlecarry,
To let awa fic a bonny lafs,
    A Highlandman to marry.

O GIN my love were yon red rofe,
    That grows upon the caftle wa'!
And I myfell a drap of dew,
    Into her bonny breaft to fa'!

Oh, there beyond expreffion bleft
    I'd feaft on beauty a' the night ;
Seal'd on her filk-faft falds to reft,
    Till flyed awa by Phœbus light.

Love is the caufe of my mourning.

BENEATH a green willow's fad ominous fhade
　　A fimple fweet youth extended was laid :
They afk'd what ail'd him, when fighing he faid,
　　O love is the caufe of my mourning !

Long lov'd I a lady, fair, gentle, and gay,
And thought myfelf loved for many a day ;
But now fhe is married, is married away,
　　And love is the caufe of my mourning ?

*　*　*　*

And when deck'd as a bride to the kirk fhe did go,
With bride-men and maidens, with pomp and with fhow,
She fmil'd in appearance—fhe fmil'd, but was woe ;
　　O love is the caufe of my mourning !

*　*　*　*

And when I had feen my love taken to bed,
And when they all kifs'd the bridegroom and bride,
Heavens ! thought I, and muft he then ly by her fide ?
　　O love is the caufe of my mourning !

Now dig me, companions, a grave dark and deep,
Lay a ftone at my head and a turf at my feet,
And O I'll ly down, and I'll take a long fleep,
　　Nor wake for ever and ever !

*　*　*　*

GOOD morrow, fair miftrefs, the beginner of ftrife ;
　　I took ye frae the begging, and made ye my wife :
It was your fair outfide that firft took my ee,
But this fall be the laft time my face ye fall fee.

Fye on ye, ill woman, the bringer o' fhame,
The abufer o' love, the difgrace o' my name;
The betrayer o' him that fo trufted in thee :
But this is the laft time my face ye fall fee.

To the ground fhall be razed thefe halls and thefe bowers,
Defil'd by your lufts and your wanton amours :
I'll find out a lady of higher degree,
And this is the laft time my face ye fall fee.

*　*　*　*

---

*　*　*　*

FALSE luve! and hae ze played me this,
　In the fimmer 'mid the flowers?
I fall repay ze back again,
　In the winter 'mid the fhowers.

Bot again, dear luve, and again, dear luve,
　Will ze not turn again?
As ze look to ither women,
　Shall I to ither men.

*　*　*　*　*　*　*

---

*　*　*　*

O MY bonny, bonny MAY,
　Will ye not rue upon me;
A found, found fleep I'll never get,
　Until I lye ayont thee,

I'll gie ze four-and-twenty gude milk kye,
    Were a' caft in ae year, MAY ;
And a bonnie bull to gang them by,
    That blude-red is his hair, MAY.

I hae nae houfes, I hae nae land,
    I hae nae gowd or fee, Sir ;
I am o'er low to be your bryde,
    Zour lown I'll never be, Sir.
      * * * * * * * * *

END OF PART SECOND.

SCOTS SONGS.

PART THIRD.

COMIC

AND

HUMOROUS SONGS.

SCOTS SONGS,

PART THIRD.

COMIC

AND

HUMOROUS SONGS.

Apron. Deary.

'TWAS early in the morning a morning of May,
 A foldier and a laffie was wauking aftray ;
 Clofe down in yon meadow, yon meadow brow,
I heard the lafs cry, My apron now,
 My apron, deary, my apron now,
 My belly bears up my apron now,
 But I being a young thing, was eafy to woo,
 Which maks me cry out, My apron now.

O had I ta'en counfel o' father or mother,
Or had I advifed wi' fifter or brother,
But I being a young thing, and eafy to woo,
It makes me cry out, My apron now,
 My apron, deary, &c.

Your apron, deary, I muft confefs,
Seems fomething the fhorter, tho' naething the lefs ;

Then had your tongue, deary, and I will prove true,
And nae mair cry out, Your apron now.
    Your apron deary, &c.——Your belly, &c.
    Then had your tongue, &c.

Auld ROB MORRIS.

MITHER.

AULD Rob Morris that wins in yon glen,
  He's the king of good fallows, and wale of auld men.
Has fourſcore of black ſheep, and fourſcore too;
Auld ROB MORRIS is the man ye maun lue.

DOUCHTER.

Had your tongue, mither, and let that abee,
For his eild and my eild can never agree:
They'll never agree, and that will be ſeen;
For he is fourſcore, and I'm but fifteen.

MITHER.

Had your tongue, doughter, and lay by your pride,
For he's be the bridegroom, and ye's be the bride:
He ſhall ly by your ſide, and kiſs ye too;
Auld ROB MORRIS is the man ye maun lue.

DOUCHTER.

Auld ROB MORRIS I ken him fou weel,
His a— ſticks out like ony peet-creel,
He's out-ſhin'd, in-knee'd, and ringle-eye'd too;
Auld ROB MORRIS is the man I'll ne'er lue.

MITHER.

Tho' auld ROB MORRIS be an elderly man,
Yet his auld brafs it will buy a new pau ;
Then, douchter, ye fhoudna be fo ill to fhoo,
For auld ROB MORRIS is the man ye maun lue.

DOUCHTER.

But auld ROB MORRIS I never will haè,
His back is fo ftiff, and his beard is grown gray :
I had titter die than live wi' him a year ;
Sae mair of ROB MORRIS I never will hear.

Auld Goodman.

LATE in an evening forth I went,
    A little before the fun ga'd down,
And there I chanc'd by accident,
    To light on a battle new begun :
A man and his wife was faen in a ftrife,
    I canna weel tell you how it began ;
But ay fhe wail'd her wretched life,
    And cry'd ever, Alake, my auld goodman.

HE.

Thy auld goodman that thou tells of,
    The country kens where he was born,
Was but a filly poor vagabond,
    And ilka ane leugh him to fcorn ;
For he did fpend and mak an end
    Of gear that his forefathers wan,

VOL. II.   B

He gart the poor ſtand frae the door,
 Sae tell nae mair of thy auld goodman.

S H E.

My heart, alake, is liken to break,
 When I think on my winſome JOHN,
His blinken ee, and gait ſae free,
 Was naething like thee, thou dozen'd drone.
His roſie face, and flaxen hair,
 And a ſkin as white as ony ſwan,
Was large and tall, and comely withal,
 And thou'lt never be like my auld goodman.

H E

Why doſt thou pleen? I thee maintain,
 For meal and mawt thou diſna want;
But thy wild bees I canna pleaſe,
 Now when our gear 'gins to grow ſcant.
Of houſehold ſtuff thou haſt enough,
 Thou wants for neither pat nor pan;
Of ſicklike ware he left thee bare,
 Sae tell nae mair o' thy auld goodman.

S H E.

Yes, I may tell, and fret my ſell,
 To think on theſe blyth days I had,
When he and I together lay
 In arms into a weel made bed:
But now I ſigh and may be ſad,
 Thy courage is cauld, thy colour wan,
Thou faulds thy feet, and fa's aſleep,
 And thoul't ne'er be like my auld goodman.

Then coming was the night fae dark,
 And gane was a' the light o' day;
The carl was fear'd to mifs his mark,
 And therefore wad nae langer ftay.
Then up he gat, and he ran his way,
 I trow the wife the day fhe wan.
And ay the o'erword o' the fray
 Was ever, *Alake, my auld goodman.*

Auld SIR SIMON the King.

SOME fay that kiffing's a fin,
 But I fay that winna ftand:
It is a moft innocent thing,
 And allow'd by the laws of the land.

If it were a tranfgreffion,
 The minifters it would reprove;
But they, their elders and feffion,
 Can do it as weel as the lave.

Its lang fince it came in fafhion,
 I'm fure it will never be done,
As lang as there's in the nation,
 A lad, lafs, wife, or a lown.

What can I fay more to commend it,
 Tho' I fhould fpeak all my life?
Yet this will I fay in the end o't,
 Let ev'ry man kifs his ain wife.

Let him kifs her, clap her, and dawt her,
 And gie her benevolence due,
And that will a thrifty wife mak her,
 And fae I'll bid farewell to you.

B 2

Auld Wife beyont the Fire.

THERE was a wife won'd in a glen,
   And she had dochters nine or ten,
That fought the house baith butt and ben,
  To find their mam a snishing.
    The auld wife beyont the fire,
    The auld wife aniest the fire,
    The auld wife aboon the fire,
    She died for lack of snishing *.

Her mill into some hole had fawn,
Whatrecks, quoth she, let it be gawn,
For I maun hae a young goodman
  Shall furnish me with snishing.
    The auld wife, &c.

Her eldest dochter said right bauld,
Fy, mother, mind that now ye're auld,
And if ye with a younker wald,
  He'll waste away your snishing.
    The auld wife, &c.

The youngest dochter gae a shout,
O mother dear! your teeth's a' out,
Besides ha'f blind, you hae the gout,
  Your mill can had nae snishing.
    The auld wife, &c.

Ye lied, ye limmers, cries auld mump,
For I hae baith a tooth and stump,

---

* Snishing, in its literal meaning, is snuff made of tobacco:
but in this song it means sometimes contentment, a husband,
love, money, &c.

And will nae langer live in dump,
By wanting o' my fnifhing.
The auld wife, &c.

Thole ye, fays PEG, that pauky flut,
Mother, if you can crack a nut,
Then we will a' confent to it,
That you fhall have a fnifhing.
The auld wife, &c.

The auld ane did agree to that,
And they a piftol-bullet gat ;
She powerfully began to crack,
To win herfelf a fnifhing.
The auld wife, &c.

Braw fport it was to fee her chow't,
And 'tween her gums fae fqueeze and row't,
While frae her jaws the flaver flow't,
And ay fhe curs'd poor ftumpy.
The auld wife, &c.

At laft fhe gae a defperate fqueeze,
Which brak the auld tooth by the neez,
And fyne poor ftumpy was at eafe,
But fhe tint hopes of fnifhing.
The auld wife, &c.

She of the tafk began to tire,
And frae her dochters did retire,
Syne lean'd her down ayont the fire,
And died for lack of fnifhing.
The auld wife, &c.

Ye auld wives, notice weel this truth,
Affeen as ye're paft mark of mouth,

Ne'er do what's only fit for youth,
　　And leave aff thoughts of fnifhing :
　　Elfe like this wife beyont the fire,
　　Your bairns againft you will confpire ;
　　Nor will ye get, unlefs ye hire,
　　A young man with your fnifhing.

Andro and his Cutty Gun.

BLYTH, blyth, blyth was fhe,
　　Blyth was fhe butt and ben ;
And weel fhe loo'd a Hawick gill,
　　And leugh to fee a tappit hen.
She took me in, and fet me down,
　　And heght to keep me lawin-free ;
But, cunning carlin that fhe was,
　　She gart me birle my bawbie.

We loo'd the liquor weel enough ;
　　But waes my heart my cafh was done,
Before that I had quench'd my drowth,
　　And laith I was to paund my fhoon.
When we had three times toom'd our ftoup,
　　And the neift chappin new begun,
In ftarted, to heeze up our hope,
　　Young ANDRO wi' his cutty gun.

The carlin brought her kebbuck ben,
　　With girdle-cakes weel toafted brown :
Weel does the canny kimmer ken
　　They gar the fcuds gae glibber down.

We ca'd the bicker aft about;
    Till dawning we ne'er jee'd our bun :
And ay the cleareſt drinker out,
    Was ANDRO wi' his cutty gun.

He did like ony mavis ſing,
    And as I in his oxter ſat,
He ca'd me ay his bonny thing,
    And mony a ſappy kiſs I gat.
I hae been eaſt, I hae been weſt,
    I hae been far ayont the ſun ;
But the blytheſt lad that e'er I ſaw,
    Was ANDRO wi' his cutty gun.

Bagrie o't.

WHEN I think on this warld's pelf,
    And how little I hae o't to myſelf ;
I ſigh when I look on my thread-bare coat,
And ſhame fa' the gear and the bagrie o't.

JOHNNY was the lad that held the plough,
But now he has got goud and gear enough ;
I weel mind the day when he was nae worth a groat,
And ſhame fa', &c.

JENNY was the laſs that mucked the byre,
But now ſhe goes in her ſilken attire ;
And ſhe was a laſs who wore a plaiden coat,
And ſhame fa', &c.

Yet a' this shall never danton me,
Sae lang's I keep my fancy free ;
While I've but a penny to pay t' other pot,
May the d—l take the gear and the bagrie o't.

Birks of Abergeldie.

I THOUGHT it ance a lonefome life,
A lonefome life, a lonefome life,
I thought it ance a lonefome life,
To ly fae lang my lane, jo :
But wha would not my cafe regret ?
Since I am curfed wi' a mate,
What once I long'd for, now I hate;
I'm quite another man, jo.

When I was full out nineteen years,
Out nineteen years, out nineteen years,
When I was full out nineteen years,
I held my head fu' high, jo ;
Then I refolv'd to tak a lafs,
Ne'er thought on what wad come to pafs,
Nor look'd in matrimony's glafs,
Till headlong down I came, jo.

Before the fatal marriage-day,
So keen was I, fo keen was I,
I refted neither night nor day,
But wander'd up and down, jo.
To pleafe her I took meikle care,
Ane wad hae thought I fought nae mair,

In the wide warld to my fhare,
But her wrapt in her gown, jo.

My ain fma' ftock did fcarce defray,
Did fcarce defray, did fcarce defray,
My ain fina' ftock did fcarce defray,
Half of the marriage-charge, jo ;
For things belanging to a houfe,
I gave till I left ne'er a fouce ;
O but I'm turned wond'rous doufe,
And filler's nae fae large, jo.

Her father, and her friends likewife,
Her friends likewife, her friends likewife,
Did had her out for fuch a prize,
I thought nae labour loft, jo.
I drefs'd myfel' from neck to heel,
And a' was for a gilded pill ;
Now I would wifh the meikle deil
Had her, and pay the coft, jo.

Her father fent a fhip to fea,
A fhip to fea, a fhip to fea,
When it returns, quoth he to me,
I'll pay you ilka plack, jo.
The fervants grumble, goodwife raves,
When hungry ftomach for them craves,
Now I am tauld by the auld knave,
The fhip will ne'er came back, jo.

Alack-a-day, what will I do,
What will I do, what will I do ?
Alack-a-day what will I do ?
The honey-month is done, jo.

My glitt'ring gold is all turn'd drofs,
And filler fcarcely will be brafs.
I've nothing but a bonny lafs,
And fhe's quite out of tune, jo.

Yet fhe lays a' the blame on me,
The blame on me, the blame on me,
Says I brought her to mifery,
This is a weary life, jo.
I'd run to the wide warld's end,
If I cou'd leave but her behind;
I'm out o' hopes fhe'll ever mend;
She's prov'd a very wife, jo.

Now, bachelors, be wife in time,
Be wife in time, be wife in time,
Tho' fhe's ca'd modeft, fair and fine,
And rich in goud and plate, jo;
Yet ye'll have caufe to curfe hard Fate,
If once fhe catch you in her net;
Your blazing ftar will foon be fet;
Then look before you leap, jo.

Bob of Dumblane.

L ASSIE, lend me your braw hemp heckle,
    And I'll lend you my ripling kame;
For fainnefs, deary, I'll gar ye keckle,
    If ye'll go dance the Bob of Dumblane.
Hafte ye gang to the ground of your trunkies,
    Bufk ye braw, and dinna think fhame;
Confider in time, if leading of monkies
    Be better than dancing the Bob of Dumblane.

Be frank, my laffie, left I grow fickle,
　And tak my word and offer again,
Syne ye may chance to repent it meikle
　Ye did not accept of the Bob of Dumblane.
The dinner, the piper, and prieft fhall be ready,
　For I'm grown dowie wi' lying my lane ;
Away then leave baith minny and dady,
　And try wi' me the Bob of Dumblane.

Butter MAY.

IN yonder town there wons a MAY,
　Snack and perfyte as can be ony,
She is fae jimp, fae gamp, fae gay,
　Sae capornoytie, and fae bonny ;
She has been woo'd and loo'd by mony,
　But fhe was very ill to win ;
She wadna hae him except he were bonny,
　Tho' he were ne'er fae noble of kin.

Her bonnynefs has been forfeen,
　In ilka town baith far and near,
And when fhe kirns her minny's kirn,
　She rubs her face till it grows clear ;
But when her minny did perceive
　Sic great inlack amang the butter,
Shame fa' that filthy face of thine,
　'Tis creefh that gars your grunzie glitter.
There's Dunkyfon, Davyfon, Robie Carneil,
The lafs wi' the petticot dances right weel.
Sing Stidrum, Stouthrum, Suthrum Stonny,
An ye dance ony mair we'fe tell Mefs JOHNY.
Sing, &c.

Blythſome Bridal.

FY let us a' to the bridal,
    For there will be lilting there,
For JOCK'S *to be married to* MAGGIE,
The laſs wi' the gowden hair.
And there will be langkail and porridge,
    And bannocks of barley-meal,
And there will be good ſawt herring,
    To reliſh a cogue of good ale.
        Fy let us, &c.

And there will be SAWNEY the ſoutar,
    And WILL wi' the meikle mou :
And there will be TAM the blutter,
    With ANDREW the tinkler I trow ;
And there will be bow'd-legged ROBIE,
    With thumbleſs KATIE's goodman ;
And there will be blue-cheeked DOWBIE,
    And LAWRIE the laird of the land.
        Fy let us, &c.

And there will be ſowlibber PATIE,
    And plucky-fac'd WAT i' th' mill,
Capper-nos'd FRANCIE, and GIBBIE
    That wons in the how o' the hill ;
And there will be ALASTER SIBBIE,
    Wha in wi' black BESSY did mool,
With ſnivling LILLY, and TIBBY,
    The laſs that ſtands oft on the ſtool.
        Fy let us, &c.

And MADGE that was buckled to STENNIE,
    And coft him grey breeks to his arſe,

Wha after was hangit for ftealing,
  Great mercy it happen'd nae warfe :
And there will be gleed GEORDY JANNERS,
  And KIRSH wi' the lily-white leg,
Who gade to the fouth for manners,
  And bang'd up her wame in Monfineg.
    Fy let us, &c.

And there will be JUDEN MECLOURIE,
  And blinkin daft BARBARA MACLEG,
Wi' flea-lugged fharney-fac'd LAWRIE,
  And fhangy-mou'd halucket MEG,
And there will be happer-ars'd NANSY,
  And fairy-fac'd FLOWRIE by name,
Muck MADIE, and fat-hippet GRISY,
  The lafs wi' the gowden wame,
    Fy let us, &c.

And there will be girn-again GIBBY,
  Wi' his glaiket wife JENNY BELL,
And meafly-fhin'd MUNGO MACAPIE,
  The lad that was fkipper himfel :
There lads, and laffes in pearlings,
  Will feaft i' the heart of the ha',
On fybows, and rifarts, and carlings,
  That are baith fodden and raw.
    Fy let us, &c.

And there will be fadges and brochen,
  With fouth of good gabbock of fkate,
Powfowdie, and drammock, and crowdie,
  And caller nowtfeet in a plate.
And there will be partens and buckies,
  And whytens and fpaldings enew,

VOL. II.   C

And fingit fheepheads, and a haggies,
  And fcadlips to fup till ye fpue.
    Fy let us, &c.

And there will be lapper'd-milk kebbucks,
  And fowens, and farles, and baps,
With fwats, and well-fcraped paunches,
  And brandy in ftoups and in caps:
And there will be mealkail and caftocks,
  And fkink to fup till ye rive;
And roafts to roaft on a brander
  Of flowks that were taken alive.
    Fy let us, &c.

Scrapt haddocks, wilks, dulfe and tangles,
  And a mill of good fnifhing to prie;
When weary with eating and drinking,
  We'll rife up and dance till we die.
    Then fy let us a' to the bridal,
      For there will be lilting there,
    For JOCK*'s to be married to* MAGGIE,
      The lafs wi' the gowden hair.

The Jolly Beggar.

THERE was a jolly beggar, and a begging he was
      bound,
And he took up his quarters into a land'art town,
  And we'll gang nae mair a roving
    Sae late into the night,
  And we'll gang nae mair a roving, boys,
    Let the moon fhine ne'er fae bright.
  And we'll gang nae mair a roving.

He wad neither ly in barn, nor yet wad he in byre,
But in ahint the ha' door, or elfe afore the fire.
 And we'll gang nae mair, &c.

The beggar's bed was made at e'en wi' good clean ftraw
  and hay,
And in ahint the ha' door, and there the beggar lay.
 And we'll gang nae mair, &c.

Up raife the goodman's dochter, and for to bar the door,
And there fhe faw the beggar ftandin i' the floor.
 And we'll gang nae mair, &c.

He took the laffie in his arms, and to the bed he ran,
O hooly, hooly wi' me, Sir, ye'll waken our goodman.
 And we'll gang nae mair, &c.

The beggar was a cunnin' loon, and ne'er a word he
  fpake,
Until he got his turn done, fyne he began to crack.
 And we'll gang nae mair, &c.

Is there ony dogs into this town? Maidén, tell me true.
And what wad ye do wi' them, my hinny and my dow?
 And we'll gang nae mair, &c.

They'll rive a' my mealpocks, and do me meikle wrang.
O dool for the doing o't! are ye the poor man?
 And we'll gang nae mair, &c.

Then fhe took up the mealpocks and flang them o'er
  the wa',
The d——l gae wi' the mealpocks, my maidenhead and a'.
 And we'll gang nae mair, &c.

I took ye for fome gentleman, at leaft the Laird of
    Brodie;
O dool for the doing o't! are ye the poor bodie?
    And we'll gang nae mair, &c.

He took the laffie in his arms, and gae her kiffes three,
And four-and-twenty hunder mark to pay the nurice-fee.
    And we'll gang nae mair, &c.

He took a horn frae his fide, and blew baith loud and
    fhrill;
And four-and-twenty belted knights came fkipping o'er
    the hill.
    And we'll gang nae mair, &c.

And he took out his little knife, loot a' his duddies fa',
And he was the braweft gentleman that was amang
    them a'.
    And we'll gang nae mair, &c.

The beggar was a cliver loon, and he lap fhoulder height,
O ay for ficken quarters as I gat yefternight.
    And we'll gang nae mair, &c.

The Humble Beggar.

IN Scotland there liv'd a humble beggar,
   He had neither houfe, nor hald, nor hame,
But he was weel liked by ilka bodie,
And they gae him funkets to rax his wame.

   A nivefow of meal, and handfow of groats,
A daad of a bannock or herring-brie,

Cauld parradge, or the lickings of plates,
Wad mak him as blyth as a beggar could be.

This beggar he was a humble beggar,
The feint a bit of pride had he,
He wad a ta'en his a'ms in a bikker
Frae gentleman or poor bodie.

His wallets ahint and afore did hang,
In as good order as wallets could be ;
A lang kail-gooly hang down by his fide,
And a meikle nowt-horn to rout on had he.

It happen'd ill, it happen'd warfe,
It happen'd fae that he did die ;
And wha do ye think was at his late-wak,
But lads and laffes of a high degree ?

Some were blyth, and fome were fad,
And fome they play'd at blind Harrie ;
But fuddenly up-ftarted the auld carle,
I redd you, good folks, tak tent o' me.

Up gat KATE that fat i' the nook,
Vow kimmer and how do ye ?
Up he gat and ca'd her limmier,
And ruggit and tuggit her cockernonic.

They houkit his grave in Duket's kirk-yard,
E'en fair fa' the companie ;
But when they were gaun to lay him i' th' yird,
The feint a dead nor dead was he.

And when they brought him to Duket's kirk-yard
He dunted on the kift, the boards did flie ;

And when they were gaun to put him i' the yird,
In fell the kift, and out lap he.

He cry'd, I'm cald, I'm unco cald,
Fu' fast ran the folk, and fu' fast ran he ;
But he was first hame at his ain ingle-fide,
And he helped to drink his ain dirgie.

Country Lafs.

ALTHO' I be but a country lafs,
Yet a lofty mind I bear—O,
And think myfell as good as thofe
That rich apparel wear—O.
Altho' my gown be hame-fpun grey,
My fkin it is as foft—O,
As them that fattin weeds do wear,
And carry their heads aloft—O.

What tho' I keep my father's fheep ?
The thing that muft be done—O;
With garlands of the fineft flow'rs
To fhade me frae the fun—O.
When they are feeding pleafantly,
Where grafs and flowers do fpring—O;
Then on a flow'ry bank at noon,
I fet me down and fing—O.

My Paifley piggy cork'd with fage,
Contains my drink but thin—O.
No wines do e'er my brain enrage,
Or tempt my mind to fin—O.

My country curds and wooden fpoon
  I think them unco fine—O;
And on a flowery bank at noon
  I fet me down and dine.—O.

Altho' my parents cannot raife
  Great bags of fhining gold—O,
Like them whofe daughters now-a-days
  Like fwine are bought and fold—O;
Yet my fair body it fhall keep
  An honeft heart within—O,
And for twice fifty thoufand crowns
  I value not a pin—O.

I ufe nae gums upon my hair,
  Nor chains about my neck—O;
Nor fhining rings upon my hands,
  My fingers ftraight to deck—O.
But for that lad to me fhall fa',
  And I have grace to wed—O,
I'll keep a jewel worth them a',
  I mean my maidenhead—O.

If canny Fortune give to me
  The man I dearly love—O,
Tho' we want gear I dinna care,
  My hands I can improve—O.
Expecting for a bleffing ftill
  Defcending from above—O;
Then we'll embrace and fweetly kifs,
  Repeating tales of love.—O.

Clout the Caldron.

HAVE you any pots or pans,
　Or any broken chandlers?
I am a tinker to my trade,
　And newly come frae Flanders,
As scant of siller as of grace,
　Disbanded, we've a bad run;
Gar tell the lady of the place,
　I'm come to clout her cauldron.
　　Fa adrie, didle, didle, &c.

Madam, if you have wark for me,
　I'll do't to your contentment,
And dinna care a single flie
　For any man's resentment;
For lady fair, though I appear
　To ev'ry ane a tinker,
Yet to yourfell I'm bauld to tell,
　I am a gentle jinker.
　　Fa adrie, didle, didle, &c.

Love JUPITER into a swan
　Turn'd for his lovely LEDA;
He like a bull o'er meadows ran,
　To carry aff Europa.
Then may not I, as well as he,
　To cheat your Argos blinker,
And win your love like mighty JOVE,
　Thus hide me in a tinkler.
　　Fa adrie, didle, didle, &c.

Sir, ye appear a cunning man,
　But this fine plot you'll fail in,

For there is neither pot nor pan
  Of mine you'll drive a nail in.
Then bind your budget on your back,
  And nails up in your apron,
For I've a tinkler under tack   ;
  That's us'd to clout my caldron.
    Fa adrie, didle, didle, &c.

Carle came o'er the Craft.

THE carl he came o'er the craft,
  And his beard new shaven,
He look'd at me, as he'd been daft,
  The carle trows that I wad hae him.
Howt awa, I winna hae him,
  Na, forsooth, I winna hae him!
For a' his beard be new shaven,
  Ne'er a bit will I hae him.

A filler broach he gae me nieft,
  To fasten on my curchea nooked,
I wor'd awi upon my breast;
  But soon, alake! the tongue o't crooked;
And sae may his, I winna hae him,
  Na, forsooth, I winna hae him,
Ane twice a bairn's a lass's jest,
  Sae ony fool for me may hae him.

The carl has nae fault but ane;
  For he has lands and dollars plenty;
But wae's me for him! skin and bane
  Is no for a plump lass of twenty.

Howt awa, I winna hae him.
   Na, forſooth, I winna hae him!
What ſignifies his dirty riggs,
   And caſh, without a man wi' them.

But ſhou'd my canker'd dady gar
   Me tak him 'gainſt my inclination,
I warn the fumbler to beware,
   That antlers dinna claim their ſtation.
Howt awa, I winna hae him!
   Na, forſooth, I winna hae him!
I'm fleed to crack the haly band,
   Sae lawty ſays, I ſhou'd nae hae him.

Caſt away Care.

CARE, away gae thou frae me,
   For I am no fit match for thee,
Thou bereaves me of my wits,
Wherefore I hate thy frantic fits :
Therefore I will care no moir,
Since that in cares comes no reſtoir;
But I will ſing hey down a dee,
And caſt doilt care away frae me.

   If I want, I care to get,
The moir I have, the moir I fret;
Love I much, I care for moir,
The moir I have I think I'm poor :
Thus grief and care my mind oppreſs,
Nor wealth nor wae gives no redreſs;
Therefore I'll care no moir in vain,
Since care has coſt me meikle pain.

Is not this warld a flidd'ry ball?
And thinks men ftrange to catch a fall!
Does not the fea baith ebb and flow?
And Fortune's but a painted fhow.
Why fhou'd men take care or grief,
Since that by thefe comes no relief?
Some careful faw what carelefs reap,
And wafters ware what niggarts fcrape.

Well then, ay learn to knaw thyfelf,
And care not for this warldly pelf:
Whether thy 'ftate be great or fmall,
Give thanks to GOD whate'er befall.
Sae fall thou than ay live at eafe,
No fudden grief fhall thee difpleafe:
Then may'ft thou fing, hey down a dee,
When thou haft caft all care frae thee.

Cock Laird.

A COCK laird fou cadgie,
 With JENNY did meet.
He haws'd her, he kifs'd her,
 And ca'd her his fweet.
Wilt thou gae alang
  Wi' me, JENNY, JENNY?
Thoufe be my ain lemmane,
  Jo JENNY, quoth he.

If I gang alang wi' ye,
 Ye mauna fail
To feaft me with caddels
 And good hacket-kail.

The deil's in your nicety,
    JENNY, quoth he,
Mayna bannocks of bear-meal
    Be as good for thee.

And I maun hae pinners,
    With pearling set round,
A skirt of puddy,
    And a waistcoat of brown,
Awa' with silk vanities,
    JENNY, quoth he,
For kurchis and kirtles
    Are fitter for thee.

My lairdship can yield me
    As meikle a year,
As had us in pottage
    And good knockit beer :
But having nae tenants,
    O JENNY, JENNY,
To buy ought I ne'er have
    A penny, quoth he.

The Borrowstoun merchants
    Will sell you on tick,
For we maun hae braw things,
    Abeit they soud break.
When broken, frae care
    The fools are set free,
When we mak them lairds
    In the Abbey, quoth she.

Dainty DAVIE.

WHILE fops in faft Italian verfe,
  Ilk fair ane's een and breaft rehearfe,
While fangs abound and fenfe is fcarce,
  Thefe lines I have indited:
But neither darts nor arrows here,
VENUS nor CUPID fhall appear,
And yet with thefe fine founds I fwear,
  The maidens are delighted.
    I was ay telling you,
    Lucky NANSY, *lucky* NANSY,
    Auld fprings wad ding the new,
    But ye wad never trow me.

Nor fnaw with crimfon will I mix,
To fpread upon my laffie's cheeks ;
And fyne th' unmeaning name prefix,
  MIRANDA, CHLOE, or PHILLIS.
I'll fetch nae fimile frae JOVE,
My height of extafy to prove,
Nor fighing—thus—prefent my love,
  With rofes eke and lilies.
    I was ay telling you, &c.

But ftay,—I had amaift forgot
My miftrefs and my fang to boot,
And that's an unco faut I wat ;
  But, NANSY, 'tis nae matter.
Ye fee I clink my verfe wi' rhyme,
And ken ye, that atones the crime ;

Forby, how fweet my numbers chyme,
    And flide away like water.
        I was ay telling you, &c.

Now ken, my reverend fonfy fair,
Thy runkled cheeks and lyart hair,
Thy half-fhut een and hodling air,
    Are a' my paffion's fewel.
Nae fkyring gowk, my dear, can fee,
Or love, or grace, or heaven in thee ;
Yet thou haft charms anew for me,
    Then fmile, and be na cruel.
        Leez me on thy fnawy pow,
        Lucky NANCY, *lucky* NANCY,
        Dryeft wood will eitheft low,
        And, NANCY, *fae will ye now.*

Troth I have fung the fang to you,
Which ne'er anither bard wad do ;
Hear then my charitable vow,
    Dear venerable NANSY.
But if the warld my paffion wrang,
And fay ye only live in fang,
Ken I defpife a fland'ring tongue,
And fing to pleafe my fancy.
        Leez me on thy, &c.

Druken Wife o' Gallowa.

DOWN in yon meadow a couple did tarrie,
    The goodwife fhe drank naething but fack and Canary.
The goodman complain'd to her friends right airly,
    O! gin my wife wad drink hooly and fairly.

Firſt ſhe drank Cronuny, and ſyne ſhe drank Garie,
And ſyne ſhe drank my bonny grey marie,
That carried me thro' the dubs and the lairie,
    O! gin, &c.

She drank her hoſe, ſhe drank her ſhoon,
And ſyne ſhe drank her bonny new gown;
She drank her ſark that cover'd her rarely,
    O! gin, &c.

Wad ſhe drink her ain things, I wadna care,
But ſhe drinks my claiths I canna weel ſpare;
When I'm wi' my goſſips, it angers me fairly,
    O! gin, &c.

My Sunday's coat ſhe has laid it a wad,
The beſt blue bonnet e'er was on my head:
At kirk and at market I'm cover'd but barely.
    O! gin, &c.

My bonny white mittens I wore on my hands,
Wi' her neighbour's wife ſhe has laid them in pawns;
My bane-headed ſtaff that I loo'd ſo dearly.
    O! gin, &c.

I never was for wrangling nor ſtrife,
Nor did I deny her the comforts of life,
For when there's a war, I'm ay for a parley.
    O! gin, &c.

When there's ony money, ſhe maun keep the purſe:
If I ſeek but a bawbie, ſhe'll ſcold and ſhe'll curſe;
She lives like a queen, I ſcrimped and ſparely.
    O! gin, &c.

A pint wi' her comers I wad her allow,
But when fhe fits down, fhe gets herfel fu',
And when fhe is fu' fhe is unco camftarie.

   O ! gin, &c.

When fhe comes to the ftreet, fhe roars and fhe rants,
Has no fear of her neighbours, nor minds the houfe wants ;
She rants up fome fool fang, like, Up your heart, C H A R L I E.

   O ! gin, &c.

When fhe comes hame, fhe lays on the lads,
The laffes fhe ca's them baith b——s and j—s,
And ca's myfel' ay ane auld cuckold carlie.

   O ! gin, &c.

For our lang Biding here.

WHEN we came to London town,
   We dream'd of gowd in gowpens here,
And rantingly ran up and down,
   In rifing ftocks to buy a fkair :
We daftly thought to row in rowth,
   But for our daffin paid right dear ;
The lave will fare the war in trouth,
   For our lang biding here.

But when we fand our purfes toom,
   And dainty ftocks began to fa',
We hang our lugs, and wi' a gloom,
   Girn'd at ftockjobbing ane and a'.
If ye gang near the South-fea houfe,
   The Whillywhas will grip your gear,
Syne a' the lave will fare the war,
   For our lang biding here.

For the fake of Somebody.

*F*O R *the fake of fomebody,*
 For the fake of fomebody;
I cou'd wake a winter-night
For the fake of fomebody.
I am gawn to feek a wife,
 I am gawn to buy a plaidy ;
I have three ftane of woo ;
 Carling is thy doughter ready?
 For the fake, &c.

BETTY, laffie, fay't thy fell,
 Tho' thy dame be ill to fhoo,
Firft we'll buckle, then we'll tell,
 Let her flyte and fyne come to :
What fignifies a mither's gloom,
 When love and kiffes come in play?
Shou'd we wither in our bloom,
 And in fimmer mak nae hay?
 For the fake, &c.

S H E.

Bonny lad, I carena by
 Tho' I try my luck wi' thee,
Since ye are content to tye
 The ha'f-merk bridal-band wi' me ;
I'll flip hame and wafh my feet,
 And fteal on linens fair and clean,
Syne at the tryfting-place we'll meet,
 To do but what my dame has done,
 For the fake, &c.

HE.

Now my lovely BETTY gives
    Confent in fick a heartfome gait,
It me frae a' my care relieves,
    And doubts that gart me aft. look blate ;
Then let us gang and get the grace ;
    For they that have an appetite
Should eat, and lovers fhould embrace ;.
    If thefe be fau'ts, 'tis Nature's wyte.
        For the fake, &c..

Fy gar rub her o'er wi' Strae.

GIN ye meet a bonny laffie,
    Gi'e her a kifs and let her gae ;.
But if ye meet a dirty hufly,
    Fy gar rub her o'er wi' ftrae,
Be fure ye dinna quit the grip.
    Of ilka joy when ye are young,.
Before auld age your vitals nip,
    And lay you twafald o'er a rung.

Sweet youth's a blyth and heartfome time ;.
    Then, lads and laffes, while 'tis May,
Gae pu' the gowan in its prime,
    Before it wither and decay.
Watch the faft minutes of delyte,
    When JENNY fpeaks beneath her breath,
And kiffes, laying a' the wyte
    On you, if fhe kepp ony fkaith.

Haith ye're ill bred, fhe'll, finiling, fay,
 Ye'll worry me, ye greedy rook ;
Syne frae your arms fhe'll rin away,
 And hide herfell in fome dark nook.
Her laugh will lead you to the place
 Where lyes the happinefs ye want,
And plainly tell you to your face,
 Nineteen nayfays are haff a grant.

Now to her heaving bofom cling,
 And fweetly toolie for a kifs :
Frae her fair finger whoop a ring,
 As taiken of a future blifs.
Thefe bennifons, I'm very fure,
 Are of the gods indulgent grant ;
Then, furly carles, whifh't, forbear
 To plague us wi' your whining cant.

Fint a crum of thee fhe fa's.

RETURN hameward, my heart, again,
 And bide where thou wait wont to be,
Thou art a fool to fuffer pain,
 For love of ane that loves not thee :
My heart, let be fick fantafie,
 Love only where thou haft good caufe ;
Since fcorn and liking ne'er agree,
 The fint a crum of thee fhe fa's.

To what effect fhou'd thou be thrall ?
 Be happy in thine ain free-will,

My heart, be never beſtial,
  But ken wha does thee good or ill :
And hame with me then tarry ſtill,
  And ſee wha can beſt play their paws,
And let the filly fling her fill,
  For fint a crum of thee ſhe fa's.

Tho' ſhe be fair, I will not feinzie,
  She's of a kin wi' mony mae :
For why? they are a felon menzie
  That ſeemeth good, and are not ſae.
My heart, take neither ſturt or wae
  For MEG, for MARJORY, or MAUSE ;
But be thou blyth, and let her gae,
  For fint a crum of thee ſhe fa's.

Remember how that MEDEA
  Wild for a ſight of JASON yied ;
Remember how young CRESSIDA
  Left TROILUS for DIOMEDE ;
Remember HELEN, as we read,
  Brought Troy from bliſs unto bare wa's ;
Then let her gae where ſhe may ſpeed,   /
  For fint a crum of thee ſhe fa's.

Becauſe ſhe ſaid, I took it ill,
  For her depart my heart was fair,
But was beguil'd ; gae where ſhe will,
  Beſhrew the heart that firſt takes care ;
But be thou merry, late and air,
  This is the final end and clauſe,
And let her feed and fooly fair,
  For fint a crum of thee ſhe fa's.

Ne'er dunt again within my breaft,
 Ne'er let her flights thy courage spill,.
Nor gie a fob, although she fneeft,
 She's faireft paid that gets her will.
She gecks as gif I meant her ill,
 When she glaiks paughty in her braws;
Now let her fnirt and fyke her fill,
 For fint a crum of thee she fa's.

Fee him, father, fee him.

O SAW ye JOHNY cumin, quo' she,.
 Saw ye JOHNY cumin;
O faw ye JOHNY cumin, quo' she,
 Saw ye JOHNY cumin;
O faw ye JOHNY cumin, quo' she,
 Saw ye JOHNY cumin;.
Wi' his blew bonnet on his head,
 And his dogie rinnin, quo' she,.
 And his dogie rinnin?

O fee him, father, fee him, quo' she,
 Fee him, father, fee him;
O fee him, father, fee him, quo' she,
 Fee him, father, fee him;
For he is a gallant lad, and a well-doin, quo' she,
 And a' the wark about the town
Gaes wi' me when I fee him, quo' she,
Gaes wi' me when I fee him.

O what will I do wi' him, quo' he,
 What will I do wi' him?

He has ne'er a coat upon his back,
　　And I hae nane to gi'e him.
I hae twa coats into my kift,
　　And ane of them I'll gi'e him;
And for a merk of mair fee
　　Dinna ftand wi' him, quo' fhe,
　　Dinna ftand wi' him.

For weel do I loe him, quo' fhe, weel do I loe him;
For weel do I loe him, quo' fhe, weel do I loe him.
O fee him, father, fee him, quo' fhe,
　　Fee him, father, fee him;
He'll ha'd the pleugh, thrafh in the barn,
　　And crack wi' me at e'en, quo' fhe,
　　And crack wi' me at e'en.

Fumbler's Rant.

COME carles a' of fumbler's ha',
　　And I will tell you of your fate,
Since we have married wives that's bra,
　　And canna pleafe them when 'tis late;
A pint we'll tak our hearts to chear;
　　What fau'ts we hae our wives can tell;
Gar bring us in baith ale and beer,
　　The auldeft bairn we hae's ourfell.

Chrift'ning of weans we are redd of,
　　The parifh prieft this he can tell;
We aw him nought but a grey groat,
　　The off'ring for the houfe we in-dwell.

Our bairns's tocher is a' paid,
    We're mafters of the gear ourfell;
Let either well or wae betide,
    Here's a health to a' the wives that's yell.

Our nibour's auld fon and the lafs,
    Into the barn amang the ftrae,
He gripp'd her in the dark beguefs,
    And after that came meikle wae.
Repentance ay comes afterhin',
    It coft the carle baith corn and hay;
We're quat of that wi' little din,
    Sick croffes haunt ne'er you nor I.

Now merry, merry may we be,
    When we think on our neighbour ROBIE,
The way the carle does, we fee,
    Wi' his auld fon and doughter MAGGIE;
Boots he maun hae, piftols, what not?
    The huffy maun hae corkit fhoon:
We are nae fae; gar fill the pot,
    We'll drink to a' the hours at e'en.

Here's health to JOHN MACKAY we'll drink,
    To HUGHIE, ANDREW, BOB, and TAM;
We'll fit and drink, we'll nod and wink,
    It is o'er foon for us to gang.
Foul fa' the cock, he'as fpilt the play,
    And I do trow he's but a fool,
We'll fit a while, 'tis lang to day,
    For a' the cocks they rave at Yool.

Since we have met, we'll merry be,
    The foremoft hame fhall bear the mell:

I'll fet me down, left I be fee,
    For fear that I fhould bear't myfell.
And I, quoth Rob, and down fat he,
    The gear fhall never me outride ;
But we'll take a foup of the barley brie,
    And drink to our ain yell fire-fide.

Green grows the Rafhes.

PEGGY.

MY Jocky blyth, for what thou'ft done,
    There is nae help nor mending ;
For thou haft jog'd me out of tune,
    For a' thy fair pretending.
My mither fees a change on me,
    For my complexion dafhes,
And this, alas ! has been with thee
    Sae late amang the rafhes.

JOCKY.

My PEGGY, what I've faid I'll do,
    To free thee from her fcouling;
Come then and let us buckle to,
    Nae langer let's be fooling;
For her content I'll inftant wed,
    Since thy complexion dafhes ;
And then we'll try a feather-bed,
    'Tis fafter than the rafhes.

PEGGY.

Then, JOCKY, fince thy love's fo true,
  Let mither fcoul, I'm eafy :
Sae lang's I live I ne'er fhall rue
  For what I've done to pleafe thee.
And there's my hand I's near complain ;
  Oh ! well's me on the rafhes :
Whene'er thou likes I'll do't again,
  And a fig for a' their clafhes.

Gaberlunzie Man.

THE pawkie auld carl came o'er the lee,
  Wi' mony good e'ens and days to me,
Saying, Goodwife, for your courtefie,
  Will you lodge a filly poor man ?
The night was cauld, the carl was wat,
And down ayont the ingle he fat ;
My doughter's fhoulders he 'gan to clap,
  And cadgily ranted and fang.

O wow ! quo' he, were I as free,
As firft when I faw this country,
How blyth and merry wad I be !
  And I wad never think lang.
He grew canty, and fhe grew fain ;
But little did her auld minny ken
What thir flee twa together were fay'ng,
  When wooing they were fae thrang.

And O ! quo' he, an ye were as black
As e'er the crown of my dady's hat,
'Tis I wad lay thee by my back,
　　And awa wi' me thou fhou'd gang.
And O ! quo' fhe, an I were as white,
As e'er the fnaw lay on the dike,
I'd clead me braw and lady like,
　　And awa' wi' thee I would gang.

Between the twa was made a plot;
They raife a wee before the cock,
And wilily-they fhot the lock,
　　And faft to the bent are they gane.
Up in the morn the auld wife raife,
And at her leifure pat on the claife;
Syne to the fervant's bed fhe gaes,
　　To fpeer for the filly poor man.

She gaed to the bed where the beggar lay,
The ftray was cauld, he was away,
She clapt her hand, cry'd, Waladay !
　　For fome of our geer will be gane.
Some ran to coffers, and fome to kifts,
But nonght was ftown that cou'd be mift ;
She danc'd her lane, cry'd, Praife be bleft !
　　I have lodg'd a leal poor man.

Since naething's awa, as we can learn,
The kirn's to kirn, and milk to earn,
Gae butt the houfe, lafs, and waken my bairn,
　　And bid her come quickly ben.
The fervant gade where the doughter lay,
The fheets was cauld, fhe was away,
And faft to her good wife 'gan fay,
　　She's aff wi' the gaberlunzie man.

O fy gar ride, and fy gar rin,
And hafte ye find thefe traytors again ;
For fhe's be burnt, and he's be flain,
    The wearifu' gaberlunzie-man.
Some rade upo' horfe, fome ran a fit,
The wife was wood, and out o' her wit :
She cou'd na gang, nor yet cou'd fhe fit,
    But ay fhe curs'd and fhe ban'd.

Mean time far hind out o'er the lee,
Fu' fnug in a glen, where nane cou'd fee,
The twa with kindly fport and glee,
    Cut frae a new cheefe a whang :
The priving was good, it pleas'd them baith,
To lo'e her for ay, he gae her his aith.
Quo' fhe, To leave thee I will be laith,
    My winfome gaberlunzie-man.

O kend my minny I were wi' you,
Ill-fardly wad fhe crook her mou',
Sick a poor man fhe'd never trow,
    After the gaberlunzie-man.
My dear, quo' he, ye're yet o'er young,
And ha' nae learn'd the beggars tongue,
To follow me from town to town,
    And carry the gaberlunzie on.

Wi' cauk and keel I'll win your bread,
And fpindles and whorles for them wha need,
Whilk is a gentle trade indeed,
    To carry the gaberlunzie on.
I'll bow my leg, and crook my knee,
And draw a black clout o'er my eye,
A cripple or blind they will ca' me,
    While we fhall be merry and fing,

E 2

Glancing of her Apron.

IN January laſt,
 On Munanday at morn,
As through the fields I paſt,
 To view the winter corn,
I looked me behind,
 And ſaw come o'er the know,
And glancing in her apron,
 With a bonny brent brow.

I ſaid, Good-morrow, fair maid,
 And ſhe right courteouſly
Return'd a beck, and kindly ſaid,
 Good-day, ſweet Sir, to you,
I ſpeir'd, my dear, how far awa
 Do ye intend to gae?
Quoth ſhe, I mean a mile or twa
 Out o'er yon broomy brae.

HE.

Fair maid, I'm thankfu' to my fate,
 To have ſick company;
For I'm ganging ſtraight that gate,
 Where ye intend to be.
When we had gane a mile or twain,
 I ſaid to her, my dow,
May we not lean us on this plain,
 And kiſs your bonny mou.

SHE.

Kind Sir, ye are a wi miſtane;
 For I am nane of theſe,

I hope you fome mair breeding ken,
   Than to ruffle womens claife :
For may be I have chofen ane,
   And plighted him my vow,
Wha may do wi' me what he likes,
   And kifs my bonny mou'.

H E.

Na, if ye are contracted,
   I hae nae mair to fay :
Rather than be rejected,
   I will gie o'er the play ;
And chufe anither will refpect
   My love, and on me rew ;
And let me clafp her round the neck,
   And kifs her bonny mou'.

S H E.

O Sir, ye are proud-hearted,
   And laith to be faid nay,
Elfe ye wad ne'er a ftarted
   For ought that I did fay ;
For women in their modefty,
   At firft they winna bow ;
But if we like your company,
   We'll prove as kind as you.

Gypfie Laddie *.

THE gypfies came to our good lord's gate,
    And wow but they fang fweetly;
They fang fae fweet, and fae very complete,
    That down came the fair lady.

And fhe came tripping down the ftair,
    And a' her maids before her;
As foon as they faw her well-far'd face,
    They cooft the glamer o'er her.

Gae tak frae me this gay mantile,
    And bring to me a plaidie;
For if kith and kin and a' had fworn,
    I'll follow the gypfie laddie.

Yeftreen I lay in a weel-made bed,
    And my good lord befide me;
This night I'll ly in a tenant's barn,
    Whatever fhall betide me.

* John Faw was chief or king of the gypfies in James IV.'s
time. James IV. about the year 1595 iffued a proclama-
tion, ordaining all fheriffs, &c. to affift John Faw in feizing
and fecuring fugitive gypfies, and that they fhould lend him
their prifons, flocks, fetters, &c. for that purpofe: charging
the lieges that none of them moleft, vex, unquiet, or trouble
the faid Faw and his company in doing their lawful bufinefs
within the realm, and in their paffing, remaining, or going
forth of the fame, under penalty: and charging all fkippers,
mafters of fhips, and mariners within our realm, at all ports
and havens to receive faid John and his company upon their
expences for furthering them furth of the realm to parts beyond fea.
        M'LAURIN's Remarkable Cafes, p. 774.

Oh! come to your bed, fays JONNY FAA,
  Oh! come to your bed, my dearly;
For I vow and fwear by the hilt of my fword,
  That your lord fhall nae mair come near ye.

I'll go to bed to my JONNY FAA,
  And I'll go to bed to my dearie;
For I vow and fwear by what paft yeftreen,
  That my lord fhall nae mair come near me.

I'll mak a hap to my JONNY FAA,
  And I'll make a hap to my dearie;
And he's got a' the coat gaes round,
  And my lord fhall nae mair come near me.

And when our lord came hame at e'en,
  And fpeir'd for his fair lady,
The tane fhe cry'd, and the other reply'd,
  She's awa wi' the gypfie laddie.

Gae faddle to me the black, black fteed;
  Gae faddle and mak him ready;
Before that I either eat or fleep,
  I'll gae feek my fair lady.

And we were fifteen well made men,
  Altho' we were nae bonny;
And we were a' put down but ane,
  For a fair young wanten lady.

Hey JENNY come down to JOCK.

JOCKY he came here to woo
  On ae feaft-day when we were fu';
And JENNY pat on her beft array,
  When fhe heard JOCKY was come that way.

Jenny she gaed up the stair,
  Sae privily to change her smock;
And ay sae loud as her mither did rair,
  Hey, Jenny, come down to Jock.

Jenny she came down the stair,
  And she came bobbin and bakin ben;
Her stays they were lac'd, and her waist it was jimp,
  And a bra' new-made manco gown.

Jocky took her be the hand,
  O Jenny, can ye fancy me?
My father is dead, and he 'as left me some land,
  And bra' houses twa or three;

And I will gie them a' to thee.
  A haith, quo' Jenny, I fear you mock.
Then foul fa' me gin I scorn thee;
  If ye'll be my Jenny, I'll be your Jock,

Jenny lookit, and syne she leugh,
  Ye first maun get my mither's content.
A weel, goodwife, and what say ye?
  Quo' she, Jock, I'm weel content.

Jenny to her mither did say,
  O mither, fetch us some good meat;
A piece of the butter was kirn'd the day,
  That Jocky and I thegither may eat.

Jocky unto Jenny did say,
  Jenny, my dear, I want nae meat;
It was nae for meat that I came here,
  But a' for the love of you, Jenny, my dear.

Then Jocky and Jenny were led to their bed,
  And Jocky he lay neist the stock;

And five or fix times ere break of day,
  He afk'd at JENNY how. fhe lik'd JOCK.

Quo' JENNY, dear JOCK, you gie me content,
  I blefs my mither for gieing confent :
And on the. next morning before the firft cock,
  Our JENNY did cry, I. dearly love JOCK.

JENNY fhe gaed up the gait,
  Wi' a green gown as fide as her fmock ;
And ay fae loud as her mither did rair,
  Vow firs ! has nae JENNY got JOCK.

JEANY, where haft thou been.

O JEANY, JEANY,. where haft thou been ?
  Father and mother. are feeking of thee,
Ye have been ranting, playing the wanton,
  Keeping of JOCKY company.
O BETTY, *I've been. to hear the mill clack,*
  Getting meal ground for the family,
As fow as it gade, I brang hame the fack,
  For the miller has taken nae mowter frae me.

Ha ! JEANY, JEANY, there's meal on your back,
  The miller's a wanton billy, and flee,
Tho' victual's come hame again hale, whatreck,
  I fear he has taken his mowter aff thee.
And, BETTY, ye fpread your linen to bleach,
  When that was done, where cou'd you be ?
Ha ! lafs, I faw ye flip down by the hedge,
  And wanton WILLY was following thee.

Ay, JEANY, JEANY, ye gade to the kirk ;
  But when it fkail'd, where cou'd thou be ?
Ye came nae hame till it was mirk,
  They fay the kiffing clerk came wi' ye.
O filly laffie, what wilt thou do ?
  If thou grow great, they'll heez thee high :
Look to your fell, if JOCK *prove true,*
  The clerk frae creepies will keep me free.

JENNY dang the weaver.

O MITHER dear, I 'gin to fear,
  Tho' I'm baith good and bonny,
I winna keep ; for in my fleep,
  I ftart and dream of JOHNY.
When JOHNY then comes down the glen,
  To woo me, dinna hinder ;
But with content gi' your confent,
  For we twa ne'er can finder.

Better to marry, than mifcarry ;
  For fhame and fkaith's the clink o't ;
To thole the dool, to mount the ftool,
  I downa bide to think o't ;
Sae while 'tis time, I'll fhun the crime,
  That gars poor EPPS gae whinging,
With haunches fow, and een fae blew,
  To all the bedrals bingeing.

Had EPPY's apron bidden down,
  The kirk had ne'er a kend it ;

But when the word's gane thro' the town,
　Alake how can fhe mend it !
Now TAM maun face the minifter,
　And fhe maun mount the pillar :
And that's the way that they maun gae,
　For poor folk hae nae filler.

Now had ye'r tongue, my doughter young,
　Replied the kindly mither,
Get JOHNY's hand in haly band,
　Syne wap your wealth togither.
I'm o' the mind, if he be kind,
　Ye'll do your part difcreetly ;
And prove a wife, will gar his life,
　And barrel run right fweetly.

JOCKY fou, JENNY fain.

JOCKY fou, JENNY fain,
　JENNY was nae ill to gain,
She was couthy, he was kind,
And thus the wooer tell'd his mind :

　JENNY, I'll nae mair be nice,
·Gi'e me love at ony price,
I winna prig for red or whyt,
Love alane can gi'e delyt.

Others feek they kenny what,
In looks, in carriage, and a' that;
Give me love for her I court :
Love in love makes a' the fport,

Colours mingled unco fine,
Common motives lang finfyne,
Never can engage my love,
Until my fancy firft approve.

It is na meat, but appetite
That makes our eating a delyt;
Beauty is at beft deceit;
Fancy only kens nae cheat.

JENNY NETTLES.

SAW ye JENNY NETTLES,
    JENNY NETTLES, JENNY NETTLES,
Saw ye JENNY NETTLES,
    Coming frae the market;
Bag and baggage on her back,
    Her fee and bountith in her lap;
Bag and baggage on her back,
    And a babie in her oxter.

I met ayont the kairney,
    JENNY NETTLES, JENNY NETTLES,
Singing till her bairny,
    ROBIN RATTLE's baftard;
To flee the dool, upo' the ftool,
    And ilka ane that mocks her,
She round about, feeks ROBIN out,
    To ftap it in his oxter.

Fy, fy! ROBIN RATTLE,
    ROBIN RATTLE, ROBIN RATTLE;

Fy, fy! Robin Rattle,
  Ufe Jenny Nettles kindly;
Score out the blame, and fhun the fhame,
  And without mair debate o't,
Tak hame your wain, make Jenny fain,
  The leel and leefome gate o't.

John Ochiltree.

HONEST man John Ochiltree;
    Mine ain auld John Ochiltree,
Wilt thou come o'er the moor to me,
  And dance as thou was wont to do?
Alake, alake, I wont to do!
  Ohon, ohon! I wont to do!'
Now won't-to-do's awa' frae me,
  Frae filly auld John Ochiltree.
Honeft man, John Ochiltree;
  Mine ain auld John Ochiltree:
Come anes out o'er the moor to me,
  And do what thou dow to do.
Alake, alake! I dow to do!
  Walaways! I dow to do!
To whoft and hirple o'er my tree,
  My bonny moor-powt, is a' I may do.

Walaways! John Ochiltree,
  For many a time I tell'd to thee,
Thou rade fae faft by fea and land;
  And wadna keep a bridle hand;

'Thou'd tine the beaft, thyfell wad die,
    My filly auld JOHN OCHILTREE.
Come to my arms, my bonny thing,
    And chear me up to hear thee fing;
And tell me o'er a' we hae done,
    For thoughts maun now my life fuftain.
Gae thy ways, JOHN OCHILTREE:
    Hae done! it has nae fae wi' me.
I'll fet the beaft in throw the land,
    She'll may be fa' in a better hand;
Even fit thou there, and drink thy fill,
    For I'll do as I wont to do ftill.

Kirk wad let me be.

I WAS anes a weel-tocher'd lafs,
    My mither left dollars to me;
But now I'm brought to a poor pafs,
    My ftepdame has gart them flee.
My father is aften frae hame,
    And fhe plays the deel with his gear;
She neither has lawtith nor fhame,
    And keeps the hale houfe in a fteer.

She's barmy-fac'd, thriftlefs and bauld,
    And gars me aft fret and repine;
While hungry, ha'f-naked and cauld,
    I fee her deftroy what is mine:
But foon I might hope a revenge,
    And foon of my forrows be free,
My poortith to plenty wad change,
    If fhe were hung up on a tree.

Quoth Ringan, wha lang time had loo'd
  This bonny lafs tenderly,
I'll tack thee, fweet May, in thy fnood,
  Gif thou wilt gae hame with me.
'Tis only yourfell that I want,
  Your kindnefs is better to me
Than a' that your ftepmother, fcant
  Of grace, now has taken frae thee.

I'm but a young farmer, its true,
  And ye are the fprout of a laird ;
But I have milk-cattle enow,
  And routh of good rucks in my yard ;
Ye fhall have naithing to fafh ye,
  Sax fervants fhall jouk to thee :
Then kilt up thy coats, my laffie,
  And gae thy ways hame with me.

The maiden her reafon employed,
  Not thinking the offer amifs,
Confented,—while Ringan o'erjoy'd,
  Receiv'd her with mony a kifs.
And now fhe fits blyth fingan,
  And joking her drunken ftepdame,
Delighted with her dear Ringan,
  That makes her goodwife at hame.

Tune, *Laſt Time I came o'er the Muir.*

YE blytheft lads, and laffes gay,
  Hear what my fang difclofes :
As I ae morning fleeping lay,
  Upon a bank of rofes,

Yonng JAMIE whiſking o'er the mead,
 By good luck chanc'd to ſpy me;
He took his bonnet aff his head,
 And ſaftly ſat down by me.

JAMIE tho' I right meikle priz'd,
 Yet now I wadna ken him;
But with a frown my face diſguis'd,
 And ſtrave away to ſend him.
But fondly he ſtill nearer preſt,
 And by my ſide down lying,
His beating heart thumped ſae faſt,
 I thought the lad was dying.

But ſtill reſolving to deny,
 An angry paſſion feigning,
I aften roughly ſhot him by,
 With words full of diſdaining.
Poor JAMIE bawk'd, nae favour wins,
 Went aff much diſcontented;
But I, in truth, for a' my ſins
 Ne'er haff ſae ſair repented.

Low down in the Broom.

MY daddy is a canker'd carle,
 He'll nae twin wi' his gear;
My minny ſhe's a ſcalding wife,
 Hads a' the houſe a-ſteer :
  But let them ſay, or let them do,
   It's a' ane to me;
  For he's low down, he's in the broom,
   That's waiting on me:

Waiting on me, my love,
He's waiting on me;
For he's low down, he's in the broom,
That's waiting on me.

My aunty KATE sits at her wheel,
And fair she lightlies me;
But weel ken I it's a' envy,
For ne'er a jo has she.
But let them, &c.

My cousin KATE was fair beguil'd
Wi' JOHNY i' the glen;
And ay sinsyne she cries, Beware
Of false deluding men.
But let them, &c.

Gleed SANDY he came west ae night,
And spier'd when I saw PATE;
And ay sinsyne the neighbours round
They jeer me air and late.
But let them, &c.

Now JENNY *she's gane down the broom,*
And it's to meet wi' PATE;
But what they said, or what they did,
'Tis needless to repeat:

But they seem'd blyth and weel content:
Sae merry mat they be;
For a constant swain has PATIE prov'd,
And nae less kind was she.

Ye'ave waited on me, my love,
Ye'ave waited on me;

E 3

Ye'ave waited lang amang the broom,
 Now I am bound to thee :

Sae let them fay, or let them do,
 'Tis a' ane to me ;
For I have vow'd to love you, lad,
 Until the day I die.

Lafs wi' a Lump of Land.

GI'E me a lafs wi' a lump of land,
 And we for life fhall gang the gither,
Tho' daft or wife, I'll never demand,
 Or black, or fair, it makesna whether.
I'm aff wi' wit, and beauty will fade,
 And blood alane is no worth a fhilling,
But fhe that's rich, her market's made,
 For ilka charm about her is killing.

Gi'e me a lafs wi' a lump of land,
 And in my bofom I'll hug my treafure ;
Gin I had ance her gear in my hand,
 Should love turn dowf, it will find pleafure.
Laugh on wha likes, but there's my hand,
 I hate with poortith, tho' bonny, to meddle,
Unlefs they bring cafh, or a lump of land,
 Theyfe ne'er get me to dance to their fiddle.

There's meikle good love in bands and bags,
 And filler and gowd's a fweet compleftion ;
For beauty, and wit, and virtue in rags,
 Have tint the art of gaining affeftion :

Love tips his arrows with woods and parks,
　　And caſtles, and riggs, and muirs, and meadows,
And naething can catch our modern ſparks
　　But well-tocher'd laſſes, or jointui'd-widows.

My Jo JANET.

SWEET Sir, for your courteſie,
　　When ye come by the Baſs then,
For the love ye bear to me,
　　Buy me a keeking-glaſs then.
Keek into the draw-well, JANET, JANET;
And there ye'll ſee your bonny ſell, my jo JANET.

Keeking in the draw-well clear,
　　What if I ſhou'd fa' in,
Syne a' my kin will ſay and ſwear,
　　I drown'd myſell for ſin.
Had the better be the brae, JANET, JANET;
Had the better be the brae, my jo JANET.

Good Sir, for your courteſie,
　　Coming through Aberdeen then,
For the love ye bear to me,
　　Buy me a pair of ſhoon then.
Clout the auld, the new are dear, JANET, JANET;
Ae pair may gain ye ha'f a year, my jo JANET.

But what if dancing on the green,
　　And ſkipping like a mawking,
If they ſhould ſee my clouted ſhoon,
　　Of me they will be tauking.

Dance ay laigh, and late at een, JANET, JANET.
Syne a' their faults will no be seen, my jo JANET.

Kind Sir, for your courtesie,
　When ye gae to the crofs then,
For the love ye bear to me,
　Buy me a pacing-horfe then.
Pace upo' your fpinning-wheel, JANET, JANET,
Pace upo' your fpinning-wheel, my jo JANET.

My fpinning-wheel is auld and ftiff,
　The rock o't winna ftand, Sir,
To keep the temper-pin in tiff,
　Employs aft my hand, Sir.
Mak the beft o't that ye can, JANET, JANET;
But like it never wale a man, my jo JANET.

My Daddy forbade, my Minny forbade.

WHEN I think on my lad, I figh and am fad,
　For now he is far frae me.
My daddy was harfh, my minny was warfe,
　That gart him gae yont the fea,
Without an eftate, that made him look blate;
　And yet a brave lad is he.
Gin fafe he come hame, in fpite of my dame,
　He'll ever be welcome to me.

Love fpeirs nae advice of parents o'er wife,
　That have but ae bairn like me,
That looks upon cafh, as naething but trafh,
　That fhackles what fhou'd be free.

And though my dear lad not ae penny had,
    Since qualities better has he ;
Abeit I'm an heirefs, I think it but fair is,
    To love him, fince he loves me.

Then, my dear JAMIE, to thy kind JEANIE,
    Hafte, hafte thee in o'er the fea,
To her wha can find nae eafe in her mind,
    Without a blyth fight of thee.
Though my daddy forbade, and my minny forbade,
    Forbidden I will not be ;
For fince thou alone my favour haft won,
    Nane elfe fhall e'er get it for me.

Yet them I'll not grieve, or without their leave,
    Gi'e my hand as a wife to thee :
Be content with a heart that can never defert,
    Till they ceafe to oppofe or be.
My parents may prove yet friends to our love,
    When our firm refolves they fee ;
Then I with pleafure will yield up my treafure,
    And a' that love orders, to thee.

The Maltman.

THE maltman comes on Munanday,
    He craves wonderous fair,
Cries, dame, come gi'e me my filler,
    Or malt ye'll ne'er get mair.
I took him into the pantry,
    And gave him fome good cock-broo,

Syne paid him upon a gantree,
  As hoſtler wives ſhould do.

When maltmen come for ſiller,
  And gaugers wi' wands o'e. ſoon,
Wives, tak them a' down to the cellar,
  And clear them as I have done.
This bewith, when cunzie is ſcanty,
  Will keep them frae making din,
The knack I learn'd frae an auld aunty,
  The ſnackeſt of a' my kin.

The maltman is right cunning,
  But I can be as ſlee,
And he may crack of his winning,
  When he clears ſcores with me :
For come when he likes, I'm ready;
  But if frae hame I be,
Let him wait on our kind lady,
  She'll anſwer a bill for me.

The Miller.

MERRY may the maid be
   That marries the miller,
For foul day and fair day
  He's ay bringing till her ;
Has ay a penny in his purſe
  For dinner and for ſupper ;
And gin ſhe pleaſe, a good fat cheeſe,
  And lumps of yellow butter.

When JAMIE firſt did woo me,
  I ſpeir'd what was his calling;
Fair maid, ſays he, O come and ſee,
  Ye're welcome to my dwelling:
Though I was ſhy, yet I cou'd ſpy
  The truth of what he told me,
And that his houſe was warm and couth,
  And room in it to hold me.

Behind the door a bag of meal,
  And in the kiſt was plenty
Of good hard cakes his mither bakes,
  And bannocks were na ſcanty;
A good fat ſow, a ſleeky cow
  Was ſtandin in the byre;
Whilſt lazy pouſs with mealy mouſe
  Was playing at the fire.

Good ſigns are theſe, my mither ſays,
  And bids me tak the miller;
For foul day and fair day
  He's ay bringing till her;
For meal and malt ſhe does na want,
  Nor ony thing that's dainty;
And now and then a keckling hen
  To lay her eggs in plenty.

In winter when the wind and rain
  Blows o'er the houſe and byre,
He ſits beſide a clean hearth ſtane
  Before a rouſing fire;
With nut-brown ale he tells his tale,
  Which rows him o'er fou nappy:
Who'd be a king—a petty thing,
  When a miller lives ſo happy?

MAGGY LAUDER.

WHA wad na be in love
   Wi' bonny MAGGIE LAUDER?
A piper met her gaun to Fife,
   And fpeir'd what was't they ca'd her;
Right fcornfully fhe anfwer'd him,
   Begone, you hallanfhaker,
Jog on your gate, you bladderfkate,
   My name is MAGGIE LAUDER

MAGGIE, quoth he, and by my bags,
   I'm fidging fain to fee thee ;
Sit down by me, my bonny bird,
   In troth I winna fteer thee ;
For I'm a piper to my trade,
   My name is ROB the Ranter,
The laffes loup as they were daft,
   When I blaw up my chanter.

Piper, quoth MEG, hae you your bags,
   Or is your drone in order ?
If you be ROB, I've heard of you,
   Live you upo' the border ?
The laffes a', baith far and near,
   Have heard of ROB the Ranter;
I'll fhake my foot wi' right goodwill,
   Gif you'll blaw up your chanter.

Then to his bags he fiew wi' fpeed,
   About the drone he twifted ;
MEG up and wallop'd o'er the green,
   For brawly could fhe frifk it.

Weel done, quoth he, play up, quoth fhe,
　　Weel bob'd, quoth Rob the Ranter,
'Tis worth my while to play indeed,
　　When I hae fick a dancer.

Weel hae you play'd your part, quoth MEG,
　　Your cheeks are like the crimfon;
There's nane in Scotland plays fae weel,
　　Since we loft HABBY SIMPSON.
I've liv'd in Fife, baith maid and wife,
　　Thefe ten years and a quarter;
Gin you fhould come to Enfter fair,
　　Speir ye for MAGGIE LAUDER.

Muirland WILLIE.

HARKEN and I will tell you how
　　Young muirland WILLIE came to woo,
Tho' he cou'd neither fay nor do;
　　The truth I tell to you.
But ay he cries, Whate'er betide,
MAGGY I'fe hae her to be my bride,
　　With a fal, dal, &c.

On his grey yade as he did ride,
Wi' durk and piftol by his fide,
He prick'd her on wi' meikle pride,
　　Wi' meikle mirth and glee,
Out o'er yon mofs, out o'er yon muir,
Till he came to her dady's door,
　　With a fal, dal, &c.

VOL. II.　　　　　　G

Goodman, quoth he, be ye within,
I'm come your doughter's love to win,
I carena for making meikle din;
  What anſwer gi' ye me?
Now, wooer, quoth he, wou'd ye light down,
I'll gie ye my doughter's love to win,
  With a fal, dal, &c.

Now, wooer, ſin' ye are lighted down,
Where do ye won, or in what town?
I think my doughter winna gloom,
  On ſick a lad as ye.
The wooer he ſtep'd up the houſe,
And wow but he was wondrous crouſe,
  With a fal, dal, &c.

I have three owſen in a pleugh,
Twa gude ga'en yades, and gear enough,
The place they ca' it Cadeneugh;
  I ſcorn to tell a lie:
Beſides, I hae frae the great laird,
A peat-pat, and a lang kail-yard,
  With a fal, dal, &c.

The maid put on her kirtle brown,
She was the braweſt in a' the town;
I wat on him ſhe did na gloom,
  But blinkit bonnilie.
The lover he ſtended up in haſte,
And gript her hard about the waſte,
  With a fal, dal, &c.

To win your love, maid, I'm come here,
I'm young, and hae enough o' gear;

And for myfell you need na fear,
 Troth try me whan you like.
He took aff his bonnet, and fpat in his chow,
He dighted his gab, and he prie'd her mou',
 With a fal, dal, &c.

The maiden blufh'd and bing'd fu law,
She had na will to fay him na,
But to her daddy fhe left it a',
 As they twa cou'd agree.
The lover he ga'e her the tither kifs,
Syne ran to her daddy, and tell'd him this,
 With a fal, dal, &c.

Your doughter wad na fay me na,
But to yourfell fhe'as left it a',
As we cou'd 'gree between us twa;
 Say, what'll ye gie me wi' her?
Now, wooer, quo' he, I hae na meikle,
But fick's I hae, ye's get a pickle,
 With a fal, dal, &c.

A kilnfu' of corn I'll gie to thee,
Three foums of fheep, twa good milk kye,
Ye's hae the wadding dinner free ;
 Troth I dow do nae mair.
Content, quo' he, a bargain be't,
I'm far frae hame, mak hafte, let's do't,
 With a fal, dal, &c.

The bridal-day it came to pafs,
Wi' mony a blythfome lad and lafs ;
But ficken a day there never was,
 Sick mirth was never feen.

This winfome couple ftraked hands,
Mefs JOHN ty'd up the marriage-bands,
   With a fal, dal, &c.

  And our bride's maidens were na few,
Wi' tap-knots, lug-knots, a' in blew,
Frae tap to tae they were bra' new,
    And blinkit bonnilie.
Their toys and mutches were fae clean,
  They glanced in our ladfes' een,
    With a fal, dal, &c.

  Sick hirdum, dirdum, and fick din,
Wi' he o'er her, and fhe o'er him;
The minftrels they did never-blin,
    Wi' meikle mirth and glee.
And ay they bobit, and ay they beck't,
And ay their wames together met,
   With a fal, dal, &c.

MAGGIE's Tocher.

THE meal was dear fhort fyne,
   We buckled us a' the gither;
And MAGGIE was in her prime,
  When WILLIE made courtfhip till her;
Twa piftols charg'd beguefs,
  To gi'e the courting-fhot;
And fyne came ben the lafs,
  Wi' fwats drawn frae the butt.

He firſt ſpeir'd at the guidman,
   And ſyne at GILES the mither,
An ye wad gie's a bit land,
   We'd buckle us e'en the gither.

My doughter ye ſhall hae,
   I'll gi'e you her by the hand;
But I'll part wi' my wife, by my fay,
   Or I part wi' my land:
Your tocher it ſall be good,
   There's nane ſall hae its maik,
The laſs bound in her ſnood,
   And Crummie wha kens her ſtaik;
Wi' an auld bedding o' claiths,
   Was left me by my mither,
They're jet-black o'er wi' fleas,
   Ye may cuddle in them the gither.

Ye ſpeak right weel, guidman,
   But ye maun mend your hand,
And think o' modeſty,
   Gin you'll not quat your land.
We are but young, ye ken,
   And now we're gaun the gither,
A houſe is but and ben,
   And Crummie will want her fother.
The bairns are coming on,
   And they'll cry, O their mither!
We'ave nouther pat nor pan,
   But four bare legs the gither.

Your tocher's be good enough,
   For that you needna fear,

Twa good ftilts to the pleugh,
  And ye yourfell maun steer :
Ye fall hae twa good pocks
  That ance were o' the tweel,
The t'ane to ha'd the grots,
  The ither to ha'd the meal :
Wi' an auld kift made o' wands,
  And that fall be your coffer,
Wi' aiken woody bands,
  And that may ha'd your tocher.

Confider well, guidman,
  We hae but barrow'd gear,
The horfe that I ride on
  Is SANDY WILSON's mare ;
The faddle's nane o' my ain,
  And thae's but barrow'd boots,
And whan that I gae hame,
  I maun tak to my coots ;
The cloak is GEORDY WATT's,
  That gars me look fae croufe ;
Come, fill us a cogue of fwats,
  We'll mak nae mair toom roofe,

I like you weel, young lad,
  For telling me fae plain,
I married whan little I had
  O' gear that was my ain.
But fin that things are fae,
  The bride fhe maun come forth,
Tho' a' the gear fhe'll hae
  'Twill be but little worth,

A bargain it maun be,.

    Fy cry on G I L F S the mither;

Content am I, quo'! fhe,

    E'en gar the hiffie come hither..

The bride fhe gade to her bed,.

    The bridegroom he cam till her;.

The fidler crap in at the fit,

    And they cuddle'd it a' the gither..

Scornfu' N a n s y..

Nansay's to the Green-wood gane,

    To hear the gowdfpink chatt'ring,.

And W I L L I E he has followed her,

    To gain her love by flatt'ring :

But a' that he cou'd fay or do,

    She geck'd and fcorned at him ;.

And ay whan he began to woo,.

    She bade him mind wha gat him,

What ails ye at my dad; quoth he,.

    My minny, or my aunty?

With crowdymoudy they fed me,.

    Langkail and rantytanty :

With bannocks of good barley-meal,.

    Of thae there was right plenty,

With chapped kail butter'd fu' weel;

    And was not that right dainty ?

Altho' my daddy was nae laird,.

    ('Tis daffin to be vaunty),

He keepit ay a good kail-yard,
   A ha'-houfe, aud a pantry ;
A good blue bonnet on his head,
   An o'erlay 'bout his craigy;
And ay until the day he died
   He raide on good fhanks-naigy.

Now wae and wonder on your fnout,
   Wad ye hae bonny NANSY ?
Wad ye compare yourfell to me,
   A docken to a tanfy ?
I hae a wooer o' my ain,
   They ca' him fouple SANDY,
And weel I wat his bonny mou'
   Is fweet like fugarcandy.

Wow, NANSY, what needs a' this din ?
   Do I not ken this SANDY ?
I'm fure the chief of a' his kin
   Was RAB the beggar randy ;
His minny MEG upo' her back
   Bare baith him and his billy ;
Will ye compare a nafty pack
   To me your winfome WILLIE ?

My gutcher left a good braid fword,
   Tho' it be auld and rufty,
Yet ye may tack it on my word,
   It is baith ftout and trufty ;
And if I can but get it drawn,
   Which will be right uneafy,
I fhall lay baith my lugs in pawn,
   That he fhall get a heezy.

I ken he's but a coward thief;
 Your titty BESS can tell him,
How with her rock she beat his beef,
 And swore that she wad fell him.
Then he lay blirting, like a sheep,
 And said he was a fau'ter;
Syne unto her did chirm and cheep,
 And asked pardon at her.

Then, bonny NANSY, turn to me,
 And so prevent all evil;
Let thy proud speeches now a'be,
 And prove somewhat mair civil;
Bid souple SANDY get him gone,
 And court his auld coal MAGGIE,
Wi' a' his duds outo'er his drone,
 And nought about his cragie.

Then NANSY turn'd her round about,
 And said, Did SANDY hear ye,
Ye wadna miss to get a clout;
 I ken he disna fear ye:
Sae had your tongue and say nae mair,
 Set somewhere else your fancy;
For as lang's SANDY's to the fore,
 Ye never shall get NANSY.

Slighted NANSY.

'TIS I have sev'n braw new gowns,
 And ither sev'n better to mak,
And yet for a' my new gowns,
 My wooer has turn'd his back.

Befides I hae feven milk-ky,
    And SANDY he has but three ;
And yet for a my good ky
    The laddie winna hae me.

My daddy's a delver of dykes,
    'My mither can card and fpin;
And I'm a fine fudgel lafs,
    And the filler comes linkin in ;
The filler comes linkin in,
    And it's fu' fair to fee,
And fifty times wow, O wow !
    What ails the lads at me ?

Whenever our bawty does bark,
    Then faft to the door I rin,
To fee gin ony young fpark
    Will l'ght and venture but in :
But never a ane will come in,
    Tho' mony a ane gaes by,
Syne far ben the houfe I rin,
    And a weary wight am I.

When I was at my firft prayers,
    I prayed but ance in the year;
I wifh'd for a handfome young lad,
    And a lad wi' muckle gear.
When I was at my neift prayers,
    I pray'd but now and than ;
I fafh'd na' my head about gear,
    If I gat but a handfome young man.

But now when I'in at my laft prayers,
    I pray on baith night and day,

And O ! if a beggar wad come,
  With that fame beggar I'd gae.
And O ! what will come o' me!
  And O ! and what'll I do ?
That fick a braw laffie as I
  Shou'd die for a wooer I trow.

Norland JOCKY.

A Southland Jenny, that was right bonny,
  Had for a fuiter a Norland Johny ;
But he was ficken a bafhful wooer,
That he cou'd fcarcely fpeak unto her ;
Till blinks o' her beauty, and hopes o' her filler,
Forced him at laft to tell his mind till her.
My dear, quoth he, we'll nae langer tarry,
Gin ye can loo me, let's o'er the muir and marry.

SHE.

Come, come awa' then, my Norland laddie,
Tho' we gang neatly, fome are mair gawdy ;
And albeit I have neither gowd nor money,
Come, and I'll ware my beauty on thee.

HE.

Ye laffes o' the fouth, ye're a' for dreffing ;
Laffes o' the north mind milking and threfhing ;
My minny wad be angry, and fae wad my dady,
Should I marry ane as dink as a lady ;
For I maun hae a wife that will rife i' the morning,
Crudle a' the milk, and keep the houfe a' fcolding,

Toolie wi' her nei'bours, and learn at my minny.
A Norland JOCKY maun hae a Norland JENNY.

SHE.

My father's only daughter, and twenty thousand pound,
Shall never be bestow'd on sic a silly clown :
For a' that I said was to try what was in ye.
Gae hame, ye Norland JOCK, and court your Norland
       JENNY.

O'er the Muir to MAGGIE.

AND I'll o'er the muir to MAGGIE,
    Her wit and sweetness call me,
Then to my fair I'll show my mind,
    Whatever may befal me.
If she love mirth, I'll learn to sing ;
    Or like the Nine to follow,
I'll lay my lugs in PINDUS' spring,
    And invocate APOLLO.

If she admire a martial mind,
    I'll sheath my limbs in armour ;
If to the softer dance inclin'd,
    With gayest airs I'll charm her ;
If she love grandeur, day and night,
    I'll plot my nation's glory,
Find favour in my prince's sight,
    And shine in future story.

Beauty can wonders work with ease,
    Where wit is corresponding ;

And braveſt men know beſt to pleaſe,
   With complaiſance abounding.
My bonny MAGGIE's love can turn
   Me to what ſhape ſhe pleaſes,
If in her breaſt that flame ſhall burn,
   Which in my boſom bleezes.

O'er the Hills and far away.

JOCKY met with JENNY fair,
   Aft by the dawning of the day;
But JOCKY now is fu' of care,
Since JENNY ſtaw his heart away :
Altho' ſhe promis'd to be true,
She proven has, alake ! unkind ;
Which gars poor JOCKY aften rue,
That e'er he loo'd a fickle mind.
   And it's o'er the hills and far away,
   It's o'er the hills and far away,
   It's o'er the hills and far away,
   The wind has blawn my plaid away.

Now JOCKY was a bonny lad
As e'er was born in Scotland fair;
But now, poor man, he's e'en gane wood,
Since JENNY has gart him deſpair.
Young JOCKY was a piper's ſon,
And fell in love when he was young,
But a' the ſprings that he cou'd play
Was, O'er the hills and far away.
   And it's o'er the hills, &c.

He fung,——When firſt my JENNY's face
I faw, ſhe ſeem'd ſae fu' of grace,
With meikle joy my heart was fill'd,
That's now, alas ! with ſorrow kill'd.
Oh ! was ſhe but as true as fair,
?Twad put an end to my deſpair.
Inſtead of that, ſhe is unkind,
And wavers like the winter wind.
        And it's o'er the hills, &c.

Ah ! cou'd ſhe find the diſmal wae,
That for her ſake I undergae,
She coud'na chuſe but grant relief,
And put an end to a' my grief :
But, oh ! ſhe is as fauſe as fair,
Which cauſes a' my ſighs and care ;
And ſhe triumphs in proud diſdain,
And takes a pleaſure in my pain.
        And it's o'er the hills, &c.

Hard was my hap, to fa' in love,
With ane that does ſo faithleſs prove !
Hard was my fate, to court a maid,
- That has my conſtant heart betray'd !
A thouſand times to me ſhe ſware,
She wad be true for evermair ;
But to my grief, alake ! I ſay,
She ſtaw my heart, and ran away.
        And it's o'er the hills, &c.

Since that ſhe will nae pity take,
I maun gae wander for her ſake,
And, in ilk wood and gloomy grove,
I'll ſighing ſing, Adieu to love.

Since she is faufe whom I adore,
I'll never truft a woman more :
Frae a' their charms I'll flee away,
And on my pipe I'll fweetly play,
 O'er hills and dales and far away,
 O'er hills and dales and far away,
 O'er hills and dales and far away,
 The wind has blawn my plaid away.

The Runaway Bride.

A LADIE and a laffie
 Dwelt in the South countrie,
And they hae caffen their claiths thegither,
 And married they wad be :
The bridal-day was fet,
 On Tifeday for to be ;
Then hey play up the rinawa' bride,
 For fhe has ta'en the gie.

She had nae run a mile or twa,
 Whan fhe began to confider,
The angering of her father dear,
 The difpleafing o' her mither ;
The flighting of the filly bridegroom,
 The weel warft o' the three ;
 Then hey, &c.

Her father and her mither
 Ran after her wi' fpeed,
And ay they ran until they came
 Unto the water of Tweed ;
And when they came to Kelfo town,
 They gart the clap gae thro',

Saw ye a lafs wi' a hood and a mantle;
   The face o't lin'd up wi' blue;
The face o't lin'd up wi' blue,
   And the tail lin'd up wi' green,
Saw ye a lafs wi' a hood and a mantle,
   Was married on Tifeday 'teen ?

Now wally fu' fa' the filly bridegroom,
   He was as faft as butter ;
For had fhe play'd the like to me,
   I had nae fae eafily quit her ;
I'd gi'en her a tune o' my hoboy,
   And fet my fancy free,
And fyne play'd up the runaway bride,
   And lutten her tak the gie.

The Country Wedding.

ROB's JOCK came to wooe our JENNIE
   On ae feaft-day when he was fow ;
She bufked her and made her bonnie
   When fhe heard JOCK was come to wooe :
   She burnifh'd her baith breaft and brow,
Made her as clear as ony clock.
   Then fpake our dame, and faid, I trow
You're come to wooe our JENNIE, JOCK !

Ay, dame, fays he, for that I yern
   To lout my head, and fit down by you :
Then fpake our dame, and faid, My bairn
   Has tocher of her awn to gi' you.
   Tee hee, quoth JENNIE, keik, I fee you ;
Minnie, this man makes but a mock.
   Why fay ye fae ? now leefe me o' you,
I come to woo your JENNIE, quoth JOCK,

My bairn has tocher of her awn,
  Although her friends do nane her lend,
A ftirk, a ftaig, an acre fawn,
  A goofe, a gryce, a clocking hen,
  Twa kits, a cogue, a kirn there ben,
A keam, but and a keaming-ftock,
  Of difhes and ladles nine or ten.
Come ye to wooe our JENNIE, JOCK?

A trough, a trencher, and a tap,
  A taings, a tullie, and a tub,
A fey-difh and a milking-cap,
  A greap into a grupe to grub,
  A fhode-fhool of a holin club,
A froath-ftick, can, a creel, a knock,
  A braik for hemp, that fhe may rub,
If ye will marry our JENNIE, JOCK.

A furm, a firlot, and a peck,
  A rock, a reel, a gay elwand,
A fheet, a happer, and a fack,
  A girdle, and a good wheel-band.
  Syne JOCK took JENNIE by the hand,
And cry'd a banquet, and flew a cock;
  They held the bridal upon land,
That was between our JENNIE and JOCK.

The bride upon her wedding went
  Barefoot upon a hemlock hill;
The bride's garter was o' bent,
  And fhe was born at Kelly-mill.
  The firft propine he hecht her till,
He hecht to hit her head a knock,
  She baked and fhe held her ftill;
And this gate gat our JENNIE, JOCK.

H 3

When ſhe was wedded-in his name,
   And unto him ſhe was made ſpouſe,
They haſted them ſoon hame again,
   To denner to the bridal-houſe.
   JENNIE ſat jouking like a mouſe,
But JOCK was kneef as ony cock;
   Says he to her, Had up your brows,
And fa' to your-meat, my JENNIE, quoth JOCK.

What meat ſhall we ſet them beforn,
   To JOCK ſervice loud can they cry,
Serve them with ſowce and ſodden corn,
   Till a' their wyms do ſtand awry:
   Of ſwine's fleſh there was great plenty;
Whilk was a very pleaſant meat;
   And garlick was a ſauce right dainty
To ony man that-pleas'd to eat.

They had ſix lavrocks fat and laden,
   With lang-kail, mutton, beef, and broſe,
A wyme of paunches tough like plaiden,
   With good May butter, milk, and cheeſe.
   JENNIE ſat up even at the meace,
And a' her friends ſat her beſide;
   They were a' ſerv'd with ſhrewd ſervice,
And ſae was ſeen upon the bride.

Out at the back-door faſt ſhe ſlade,
   And loos'd a buckle wi' ſome bends,
She cackied JOCK for a' his pride,
   And jawed out at baith the ends;
   So ſtoutly her mother her defends,
And ſays, My bairn's looſe in the dock,
   It comes o' cauld, to make it kend;
'Think nae ill o' your JENNIE, JOCK,

Now dame, fays he, your daughter I've married,
   Altho' you hold it never fo teugh;
And friends fhall fee fhe's nae mifcarried;
   For I wat-I have gear enough:
   An auld ga'd glyde fell owre the heugh,.
A cat, a cunnin, and a cock;
   I wanted eight oufen, though I had the pleugh:
May this not ferve your JENNIE; quoth JOCK?

I have good fire for winter-weather;
   A cod o' caff wou'd fill a cradle,.
A halter, and a good hay-tether,
   A duck about the doors to paddle;
   The pannel of a good auld faddle,
And ROB my emme hecht me a fock,.
   Twa lovely lips to lick a laddle;
Gif JENNIE and I agree, quoth JOCK.

A treen fpit, a ram-horn fpoon,
   A pair o' boots o' barked leather,
All graith that's meet to coble fhoon,
   A thraw-crook for to twine a tether;
   A fword, a fweel, a fwine's bladder,.
A trump o' fteel, a feather'd lock,.
   An auld fcull-hat for winter-weather,
And meikle mair, my JENNIE, quoth JOCK.

I have a cat to catch a moufe,
   A girfe-green cloak, but it will ftenzie;
A pitch-fork to defend the houfe,
   A pair of branks, a bridle renzie;
   Of a' our ftore we need not plenzie,
Ten thoufand flechs intil a pock;
   And is not this a wakerife menzie,
To gae to bed wi' JENNIE and JOCK?

Now when their dinner they had done,
   Then JOCK himfell began t' advance;
He bad the piper play up foon,
   For, be his troth, he wou'd gae dance.
The piper piped till's wyme gripped,
   And a' the rout began to revel:
The bride about the ring fhe fkipped,
   Till out ftarts baith the carle and cavel.

Weel danc'd, DICKIE, ftand afide, SANDIE;
   Weel danc'd EPPIE and JENNIE!
He that tynes a ftot o' the fpring,
   Shall pay the piper a pennie.
Weel danc'd, HUGH FISHER;
Come, take out the bride and kifs her;
Weel danc'd, BESSIE and STE'EN!
Now fick a dance was never feen
   Since *Chrift's Kirk on the green.*

Rock and wee Pickle Tow.

THERE was an auld wife had a wee pickle tow,
   And fhe wad gae try the fpinning o't,
But louten her down, her rock took a low,
   And that was an ill beginning o't;
She lap and fhe grat, fhe flet and fhe flang,
She trow and fhe drew, fhe ringled, fhe rang,
She choaked fhe bocked, and cried, Let me hang,
   That ever I try'd the fpinning o't.

I hae been a wife thefe threefcore of years,
   And never did try the fpinning o't;

But how I was farked foul fa' them that fpeirs,
 For it minds me o' the beginning o't;
The women now a-days are turned fae bra',
That ilk ane maun hae a fark, fome maun hae twa,
But the warld was better whan feint ane ava,
 But a wee rag at the beginning o't.

Foul fa' them that e'er advis'd me to fpin,
 For it minds me o' the beginning o't;
I might well have ended as I had begun,
 And never had try'd the fpinning o't.:
But they fay fhe's a wife wife wha kens her ain weird;
I thought ance a day it wad never be fpeir'd,
How loot you the low tak the rock by the beard,.
 Whan you gaed to try the fpinning o't?

The fpinning, the fpinning, it gars my heart fab,
 Whan I think on the beginning o't;
I thought ance in a day to 'ave made a wab,
 And this was to 'ave been the beginning o't;
But had I nine doughters, as I hae but three,
The fafeft and foundeft advice I wad gie,
That they frae fpinning wad keep their hands free,
 For fear o' an ill beginning o't.

But in fpite of my counfel if they wad needs run
 The dreary fad tafk o' the fpinning o't,
Let them feek out a loun place at the heat o' the fun,
 Syne venture on the beginning o't:
For, O do as I've done, alake and vow,
To bufk up a rock at the cheek of a low,
They'd fay, that I had little wit in my pow,
 And as little I've done wi' the fpinning o't.

Same Tune.

I HAE a green purfe and a wee pickle gowd,
 A bonny piece land, and planting on't,
It fattens my flocks, and my barns it has ftowed;
 But the beft thing of a's yet wanting on't:
To grace it, and trace it, and gi'e me delight,
To blefs me, and kifs me, and comfort my fight,
With beauty by day, and kindnefs by night,
 And nae mair my lane gang faunt'ring on't.

My CHIRSTY is charming, and good as fhe's fair;
 Her een and her mouth are inchanting fweet;
She fmiles me on fire, her frowns gi'e defpair;
 I love while my heart gaes panting wi't.
Thou faireft and deareft delight of my mind,
Whofe gracious embraces by Heav'n were defign'd
For happieft tranfports, and bliffes refin'd,
 Nae langer delay thy granting fweet.

For thee, bonny CHIRSTY, my fhepherds and hynds
 Shall carefully make the year's dainties thine;
Thus freed frae laigh care, while love fills our minds,
 Our days fhall with pleafure and plenty fhine.
Then hear me, and chear me with fmiling confent,
Believe me, and give me no caufe to lament,
Since I ne'er can be happy till thou fay Content,
 I'm pleas'd with my JAMIE, and he fhall be mine.

To the Tune of *Saw ye nae my* PEGGY.

COME, let's hae mair wine in,
 BACCHUS hates repining,
VENUS loes nae dwining,
 Let's be blyth and free.

Away with dull, Here t'ye, Sir,
Your miftrefs, ROBIE, gi'es her,
We'll drink her health wi' pleafure,
 Wha's belov'd by thee.

Then let PEGGY warm ye,
That's a lafs can charm ye,
And to joys alarm ye,
 Sweet is fhe to me.
Some angel ye wad ca' her,
And never wifh ane brawer,
If ye bareheaded faw her,
 Kiltit to the knee.

PEGGY a dainty lafs is;
Come, let's join our glaffes,
And refrefh our haafes,
 With a health to thee.
Let coofs their cafh be clinking,
Be ftatefmen tint in thinking,
While we with love and drinking
 Gie our cares the lie.

Spinning Wheel.

AS I fat at my fpinning-wheel,
 A bonny lad was paffing by:
I view'd him round, and lik'd him weel,
 For trouth he had a glancing eye.
 My heart new panting 'gan to feel,
 But ftill I turn'd my fpinning-wheel.

With looks all kindnefs he drew near,
And ftill mair lovely did appear;
And round about my flender waift
He clafp'd his arms, and me embrac'd :
    To kifs my hand fyne down did kneel,
    As I fat at my fpinning-wheel.

My milk-white hands he did extol,
And prais'd my fingers lang and fmall,
And faid, there was nae lady fair
That ever cou'd with me compare.
    Thefe words into my heart did fteal,
    But ftill I turn'd my fpinning-wheel.

Altho' I feemingly did chide,
Yet he wad never be deny'd,
But ftill declar'd his love the mair,
Untill my heart was wounded fair :
    That I my love cou'd fcarce conceal,
    Yet ftill I turn'd my fpinning-wheel.

My hanks of yarn, my rock and reel,
My winnels and my fpinning-wheel;
He bid me leave them all with fpeed,
And gang with him to yonder mead :
    My yielding heart ftrange flames did feel,
    Yet ftill I turn'd my fpinning-wheel.

About my neck his arm he laid,
And whifper'd, Rife, my bonny maid,
And with me to yon haycock go,
I'll teach thee better wark to do.
    In trouth I loo'd the motion weel,
    And loot alane my fpinning-wheel.

Amang the pleafant cocks of hay,
Then with my bonny lad I lay;
What laffie, young and faft as I,
Cou'd fick a handfome lad deny?
 Thefe pleafures I cannot reveal,
 That far furpaft the fpinning-wheel.

Steer her up and had her gawin.

O STEER her up, and had her gawin,
 Her mither's at the mill, jo;
But gin fhe winna tak a man,
 E'en let her tak her will, jo.
Pray thee, lad, leave filly thinking,
 Caft thy cares of love away;
Let's our forrows drown in drinking,
 'Tis daffin langer to delay.

See that fhining glafs of claret,
 How invitingly it looks;
Tak it aff, and let's hae mair o't,
 Pox on fighing, trade, and books.
Let's hae mair pleafure while we're able,
 Bring us in the meikle bowl,
Place't on the middle of the table,
 And let the wind and weather gowl.

Call the drawer, let him fill it
 Fou' as ever it can hold:
O tak tent ye dinna fpill it,
 'Tis mair precious far then gold.
By you've drunk a dozen bumpers,
 BACCHUS will begin to prove,
  VOL. II.   I

Spite of V E N U S and her mumpers,
　Drinking better is than love.

Sleepy Body.

S Omnolente, quæso, repente
　Vigila, vivat, me tange.
Somnolente, quæso, repente
Vigila, vive, me tange.
Cum me amliebas,
　Videri solebas
Amoris negotiis aptus;
At factus moritus,
　In lecto sopitus
Somno es, haud amore, tu captus.

　O sleepy body,
　And drowsy body,
O wiltuna waken and turn thee?
　To drivel and draunt,
　While I sigh and gaunt,
Gives me good reason to scorn thee.

　When thou shouldst be kind,
　Thou turns sleepy and blind,
And snoters and snores far frae me.
　Wae light on thy face,
　Thy drowsy embrace
Is enough to gar me betray thee.

Sir JOHN MALCOLM.

KEEP ye weel frae Sir JOHN MALCOLM, Igo
and ago,
If he's a wife man, I miftak him, Iram coram dago.
Keep ye weel frae SANDIE DON, Igo and ago,
He's ten times dafter than Sir JOHN, Iram coram dago.

To hear them of their travels talk,
To gae to London's but a walk:
I hae been at Amfterdam,
Where I faw mony a braw madam.

To fee the wonders of the deep,
Wad gar a man baith wail and weep;
To fee the Leviathans flip,
And wi' their tail ding o'er a fhip.

Was ye e'er in Crail town?
Did ye fee Clark DISHINGTOUN?
His wig was like a drouket hen,
And the tail o't hang down,
like a meikle maan lang draket gray goofe-pen.

But for to make ye mair enamour'd,
He has a glafs in his beft chamber;
But forth he ftept unto the door,
For he took pills the night before.

There's my thumb I'll ne'er beguile thee.

MY fweeteft MAY, let love incline thee,
T' accept a heart which he defigns thee;
And, as your conftant flave regard it,
Syne for its faithfulnefs reward it.

'Tis proof a-shot to birth or money,
But yields to what is sweet and bonny;
Receive it then with a kiss and a smily,
There's my thumb it will ne'er beguile ye.

How tempting sweet these lips of thine are!
Thy bosom white, and legs sae fine are,
That, when in pools I see thee clean 'em,
They carry away my heart between 'em.
I wish, and I wish, while it gaes duntin,
O gin I had thee on a mountain,
Tho' kith and kin and a' shou'd revile thee,
There's my thumb I'll ne'er beguile thee.

Alane through flow'ry hows I dander,
Tenting my flocks left they should wander;
Gin thou'll gae alang, I'll dawt thee gaylie,
And gi' ye my thumb I'll ne'er beguile thee.
O my dear lassie, it is but daffin,
To had thy wooer up ay niff-naffin.
That Na, na, na, I hate it most vilely,
O say Yes, and I'll ne'er beguile thee.

Tarry Woo.

TARRY woo, tarry woo,
    Tarry woo is ill to spin,
Card it well, card it well,
Card it well ere ye begin.
When 'tis carded, row'd and spun,
Then the work is haflens done;
But when woven, dreft and clean,
It may be cleading for a queen.

Sing, my bonny harmlefs fheep,
That feed upon the mountains fteep;
Bleating fweetly as ye go
Thro' the winter's froft and fnow;
Hart and hynd and fallow deer,
No be ha'f fo ufeful are;
Frae kings to him that ha'ds the plow,
Are all oblig'd to tarry woo.

Up ye fhepherds, dance and fkip,
O'er the hills and valleys trip,
Sing up the praife of tarry woo,
Sing the flocks that bear it too;
Harmlefs creatures without blame,
That clead the back and cram the wame,
Keep us warm and hearty fou;
Leefe me on the tarry woo.

How happy is a fhepherd's life,
Far frae courts and free of ftrife,
While the gimmers bleat and bae,
And the lambkins anfwer mae?
No fuch mufic to his ear,
Of thief or fox he has no fear;
Sturdy kent and colly too,
Well defend the tarry woo.

He lives content, and envies none;
Not even a monarch on his throne,
Tho' he the royal fcepter fways,
Has not fweeter holydays.
Who'd be a king, can ony tell,
When a fhepherd fings fae well;
Sings fae well, and pays his due,
With honeft heart and tarry woo?

I 3

Tak your auld Cloak about you.

IN Winter when the rain rain'd cauld,
  And froft and fnaw on ilka hill,
And Boreas, wi' his blafts fae bauld,.
  Was threat'ning a' our ky to kill :
Then BELL, my wife, wha lo'es nae ftrife,.
  She faid to me right haftily,
Get up, goodman, fave Cromy's life,.
  And tak your auld cloak about ye.

O BELL, *why doft thou flyte and fcorn ?*
  Thou kenft my cloak is very thin :
It is fo bare and overworne,
  A cricke he thereon cannot rin :
Then I'll noe longer borrow nor lend,.
  For ance I'll new apparel'd be,
To-morrow I'll to town and ffend,.
  For I'll have a new cloak about me.

My Cromie is an ufeful cow,
  And fhe is come of a good kine ;
Aft has fhe wet the bairns' mou,
  And I am laith that fhe fhou'd tyne ;
Get up, goodman, it is fou time,
  The fun fhines in the lift fae hie ;.
Sloth never made a gracious end,
  Gae tak your auld cloak about ye.

My cloak was anes a good grey cloak,
  When it was fitting for my wear ;.
But now its fcantly worth a groat,
  For I have worn't this thirty year ;

Let's fpend the gear that we have won,
  We little ken the day we'll die;
Then I'll be proud, fince I have fworn
  To have a new cloak about me.

In days when our King ROBERT rang,
  His trews they coft but ha'f-a-crown;
He faid they were a groat o'er dear,
  And ca'd the taylor thief and lown;
He was the king that wore a crown,
  And thou'rt a man of laigh degree;
'Tis pride puts a' the country down,
  Sae tak thy auld cloak about thee.

Every land has its ain lough,
  Ilk kind of corn it has its hool;
I think the warld is a' run wrang,
  When ilka wife her man wad rule;
Do ye not fee ROB, JOCK and HAB,
  As they are girded gallantly,
While I fit hurklen in the afe?
  I'll have a new cloak about me.

Goodman, I wat 'tis thirty years
  Since we did ane anither ken;
And we have had between us twa,
  Of lads and bonny laffes ten:
Now, they are women grown and men,
  I wifh and pray well may they be;
And if you prove a good hufband,
  E'en tak your auld cloak about ye.

BELL, my wife fhe lo'es na ftrife;
  But fhe wad guide me if fhe can,

And to maintain an eafy life,
    I aft maun yield; tho' I'm goodman:
Nought's to be won at woman's hand,
    Unlefs ye gi'e her a' the plea;
Then I'll leave aff where I began,
    And tak my auld cloak about me.

TIBBY FOWLER of the Glen.

TIBBY has a ftore of charms,
    Her genty fhape our fancy warms;
How ftrangely can her fma' white arms
    Fetter the lads who look but at her!
Frae her ancle to her flender waift,
    Thefe fweets conceal'd invite to dawt her;
Her rofy cheek and rifing breaft
    Gar ane's mouth gufh bowt fu' of water.

NELLY's gawfy, faft, and gay,
Frefh as the lucken flowers in May;
Ilk ane that fees her, cryes, Ah, hey!
    She's bonny! Oh! I wonder at her.
The dimples of her chin and cheek,
    And limbs fae plump invite to dawt her;
Her lips fae fweet, and fkin fae fleek,
    Gar mony mouths befides mine water.

Now ftrike my finger in a bore,
My wifou wi' the maiden fhore,
Gin I can tell whilk I am for,
    When thefe twa ftars appear the gither,

O Love! why didſt thou gi'e thy fires
   Sae large, while we're oblig'd to neither ?
Our ſpacious ſauls' immenſe deſires,
   And ay be in a hankerin ſwither.

TIBBY's ſhape and airs are fine,
And NELLY's beauties are divine ;
But ſince they canna baith be mine,
   Ye gods, give ear to my petition :
Provide a good lad for the tane,
   But let it be with this proviſion,
I get the other to my lane,
   In proſpect, *plano*, and fruition.

This is no mine ain houſe.

THIS is no mine ain houſe,
   I ken by the rigging o't ;
Since with my love I've changed vows,
   I dinna like the bigging o't.
For now that I'm young ROBIE's bride,
And miſtreſs of his fire-ſide,
Mine ain houſe I like to guide,
   And pleaſe me wi' the trigging o't.

Then farewell to my father's houſe,
   I gang where love invites me ;
The ſtricteſt duty this allows,
   When love with honour meets me.
When HYMEN moulds me into ane,

My Robie's nearer than my kin,.
And to refufe him were a fin,
 Sae lang's he kindly treats me.

When I am in mine ain houfe,
 True love fhall be at hand ay,
To make me ftill a prudent fpoufe,.
 And let my man command ay ;
Avoiding ilka caufe of ftrife,
The common peft of married life,
That makes ane wearied of his wife,
 And breaks the kindly band ay.

'   Todlen hame.

WHAN I've a faxpence under my thum,.
 Then I'll get credit in ilka town :
But ay whan I'm poor they bid me gang by ;.
O ! poverty parts good company.
 Todlen hame, todlen hame,
 Cou'dna my love come todlen hame ?

 Fair fa' the goodwife, and fend her good fale,
She gi'es us white bannocks to drink her ale,.
Syne if her typpony chance to be fma',
We'll tak a good fcour o't, and ca't awa'.
 Todlen hame, todlen hame,
 As round as a neep come todlen hame.

 My kimmer and I lay down to fleep,
And twa pint ftoups at our bed-feet ;

And ay when we waken'd we drank them dry :
What think you of my wee kimmer and I ?
    Todlen butt and todlen ben,
    Sae round as my love comes todlen hame.

Leez me on liquor, my todlen dow,
Ye're ay fae good-humour'd when weeting your mou' ;
When fober fae four, ye'll fight wi' a flee,
That it's a blyth fight to the bairns and me,
    Todlen hame, todlen hame,
    When round as a neep ye come todlen hame.

What's that to you?

MY JEANY and I have toil'd
    The live-lang fummer-day,
Till we amaift were fpoil'd
    At making of the hay :
Her kurchy was of holland clear,
    Ty'd on her bonny brow ;
I whifper'd fomething in her ear,
    But what's that to you ?

Her ftockings were of Kerfy green,
    As tight as ony filk :
O fick a leg was never feen,
    Her fkin was white as milk ;
Her hair was black as ane could wifh,
    And fweet fweet was her mou ;
Oh ! JEANY daintily can kifs,
    But what's that to you ?

The rofe and lily baith combine
  To make my JEANY fair,
There is no bennifon like mine,
  I have amaift nae care ;
Only I fear my JEANY's face
  May caufe mae men to rue,
And that may gar me fay, Alas !
  But what's that to you ?

Conceal thy beauties if thou can,
  Hide that fweet face of thine,
That I may only be the man
  Enjoys thefe looks divine.
O do not proftitute, my dear,
  Wonders to common view,
And I, with faithful heart, fhall fwear
  For ever to be true.

King SOLOMON had wives enew,
  And mony a concubine ;
But I enjoy a blifs mair true ;
  His joys were fhort of mine :
And JEANY's happier than they,
  She feldom wants her due ;
All debts of love to her I'll pay,
  And what's that to you ?

Were na my Heart light I wad die.

THERE was ance a MAY, and fhe loe'd na men,
  She biggit her bonny bow'r down in yon glen ;
But now fhe cries dool ! and a well-a-day !
Come down the green gate, and come here away.
  But now fhe cries, &c.

When bonny young JOHNY came o'er the fea,
He faid he faw naething fae lovely as me;
He hecht me baith rings and mony bra things;
And were na my heart light I wad die.
    He hecht me, &c.

He had a wee titty that loed na me,
Becaufe I was twice as bonny as fhe;
She rais'd fick a pother 'twixt him and his mother,
That were na my heart light I wad die.
    She rais'd, &c.

The day it was fet, and the bridal to be,
The wife took a dwam, and lay down to die;
She main'd and fhe grain'd out of dolour and pain,
Till he vow'd he never wad fee me again.
    She main'd, &c.

His kin was for ane of a higher degree,
Said, What had he to do with the like of me!
Albeit I was bonny, I was na for JOHNY:
And were na my heart light I wad die.
    Albeit I was bonny, &c.

They faid I had neither cow nor caff,
Nor dribbles of drink rins throw the draff,
Nor pickles of meal rins throw the mill-eye;
And were na my heart light I wad die.
    Nor pickles of, &c.

His titty fhe was baith wylie and flee,
She fpy'd me as I came o'er the lee;
And then fhe ran in and made a loud din,
Believe your ain een, an ye trow na me.
    And then fhe, &c.

His bonnet ſtood ay fu' round on his brow ;
His auld ane looks ay as well as ſome's new :
But now he lets't wear ony gate it will hing,
And caſts himſelf dowie upo' the corn-bing.
    But now he, &c.

And now he gaes drooping about the dykes,
And a' he dow do is to hund the tykes :
The live-lang night he ne'er ſteeks his eye,
And were na my heart light I wad die.
    The live-lang, &c.

Were I young for thee, as I hae been,
We ſhou'd hae been galloping down on yon green,
And linking it on the lily-white lee ;
And wow gin I were but young for thee.
    And linking, &c.

Where will our Goodman ly?

H E.

WHERE wad bonnie ANNIE ly?
    Alane nae mair ye maun ly ;
Wad ye a goodman try ?
    Is that the thing ye're lacking !

S H E.

Can a laſs ſae young as I,
Venture on the bridal-tye,
Syne down with a goodman ly ?
    I'm flee'd he keep me wauking.

H E.

Never judge until ye try,
Mak me your goodman, I
Shanna hinder you to ly,
    And fleep till ye be weary.

S H E.

What if I fhou'd wauking ly,
When the hoboys are gawn by,
Will ye tent me when I cry,
    My dear, I'm faint and iry?

H E.

In my bofom thou fhalt ly,
When thou wakrife art, or dry,
Healthy cordial ftanding by,
    Shall prefently revive thee.

S H E.

To your will I then comply,
Join us, prieft, and let me try,
How I'll wi' a goodman ly,
    Wha can a cordial gi'e me.

Widow, are ye waking?

OWHA's that at my chamber-door?
    " Fair widow, are ye waking?"
Auld carl, your fuit give o'er,
    Your love lyes a' in tawking.

K 2

Gi'e me a lad that's young and tight,
　　Sweet like an April meadow ;
'Tis fick as he can blefs the fight,
　　And bofom of a widow.

" O widow, wilt thou let me in ?
　　" I'm pawky, wife, and thrifty,
" And come of a right gentle kin ;
　　" I'm little mair than fifty."
Daft carle, dit your mouth,
　　What fignifies how pawky,
Or gentle-born ye be,—but youth,.
　　In love ye're but a gawky.

" Then, widow, let thefe guineas fpeak,.
　　" That powerfully plead clinkan;
" And if they fail, my mouth I'll fteek,
　　" And nae mair love will think on."
Thefe court indeed, I maun confefs,
　　I think they mak you young, Sir,.
And ten times better can exprefs
　　Affection, than your tongue, Sir,

Wap at the Widow, my Laddie.

THE widow can bake, and the widow can brew,
　　The widow can fhape and the widow can few,
And mony bra things the widow can do ;
　　Then have at the widow, my laddie.
With courage attack her baith early and late,
　　To kifs her and clap her you manna be blate ;
Speak well and do better, for that's the beft gate
　　To win a young widow, my laddie.

The widow she's youthfu', and never ae hair
The war of the wearing, and has a good skair
Of every thing lovely ; she's witty and fair,
    And has a rich jointure, my láddie ?
What cou'd you with better your pleafure to crown,
Than a widow, the bonnieft toaft in the town,
Wi' naething but draw in your ftool and fit down,
    And fport wi' the widow, my laddie ?

Then till 'er and kill 'er wi' courtefie dead,
Tho' ftark love and kindnefs be a' ye can plead ;
Be heartfome and airy, and hope to fucceed
    Wi' a bonny gay widow, my laddie.
Strike iron while 'tis het, if ye'd have it to wald;
For Fortune ay favours the active and bauld,
But ruins the wooer that's thowlefs and cauld,
    Unfit for the widow, my laddie.

WILLIE was a wanton Wag.

WILLIE was a wanton wag,
    The blytheft lad that e'er I faw,
At bridals ftill he bore the brag,
    And carried ay the gree awa' :
His doublet was of Zetland fhag,
    And wow ! but WILLIE he was braw;
And at his fhoulder hang a tag,
    That pleas'd the laffes beft of a'.

He was a man without a clag,
    His heart was frank without a flaw;

K 3

And ay whatever W I L L I E faid,
   It was ftill hadden as a law.
His boots they were made of the jag,
   When he went to the Weaponfhaw,
Upon the green nane durft him brag,
   The fiend a ane amang them a'.

And was not W I L L I E well worth gowd?
   He wan the love of great and fma';
For after he the bride had kifs'd,
   He kifs'd the laffes hale-fale a'.
Sae merrily round the ring they row'd,
   When be the hand he led them a',
And fmack on fmack on them beftow'd,
   By virtue of a ftanding law.

And was nae W I L L I E a great lown,
   As fhyre a lick as e'er was feen?
When he danc'd wi' the laffes round,
   The bridegroom fpeir'd where he had been,
Quoth W I L L I E, I've been at the ring,
   Wi' bobbing, faith, my fhanks are fair;
Gae ca' your bride and maiden in,
   For W I L L I E he dow do nae mair.

Then reft ye, W I L L I E, I'll gae out,
   And for a wee fill up the ring.
But, fhame light on his fouple fnout,
   He wauted W I L L I E's wanton fling.
Then ftraight he to the bride did fare,
   Says, Well's me on your bonny face;
Wi' bobbing W I L L I E's fhanks are fair,
   And I'm come out to fill his place.

Bridegroom, fhe fays, you'll fpoil the dance,
  And at the ring you'll ay be lag,
Unlefs, like WILLIE, ye advance:
  O! WILLIE has a wanton leg;
For wi't he learns us a' to fteer,
  And foremoft ay bears up the ring;
We will find nae fick dancing here,
  If we want WILLIE's wanton fling.

Woo'd and married and a'.

WOO'D and married and a',
  Woo'd and married and a';
Was fhe nae very weel aff
  Was woo'd and married and a'.
The Bride came out of the byre,
  And O as fhe dighted her cheeks,
Sirs, I'm to be married the night,
  And has neither blankets nor fheets,
  Has neither blankets nor fheets,
  Nor fcarce a coverlet too;
The bride that has a' to borrow,
  Has e'en right meikle ado.
    Woo'd, and married, &c.

Out fpake the bride's father,
  As he came in frae the plough;
O had ye're tongue, my doughter,
  And ye's get gear enough;
The ftirk that ftands i' the' tether,
  And our bra' bafin'd yad,

Will carry ye hame your corn,
  What wad ye be at, ye jad?
  Woo'd, and married, &c.

Out fpake the bride's mither,
  What d---l needs a' this pride;
I had nae a plack in my pouch
  That night I was a bride;
My gown was linfy-woolfy,
  And ne'er a fark ava;
And ye hae ribbons and bufkins,
  Mae than ane or twa.
    Woo'd, and married, &c.

What's the matter, quo WILLIE,
  Tho' we be fcant o' claiths,
We'll creep the nearer the gither,
  And we'll fmore a' the fleas:
Simmer is coming on,
  And we'll get teats of woo;
And we'll get a lafs o' our ain,
  And fhe'll fpin claiths enew.
    Woo'd, and married, &c.

Out fpake the bride's brither,
  As he came in wi' the kie;
Poor WILLIE had ne'er a ta'en ye,
  Had he kent ye as weel as I;
For you're baith proud and faucy,
  And no for a poor man's wife;
Gin I canna get a better,
  Ife never tak ane i' my life.
    Wood, and married, &c.

Out fpake the bride's fifter,
  As fhe came in frae the byre;

O gin I were but married,
  It's a' that I defire :
But we poor fo'k maun live fingle,
  And do the beft we can;
I dinna care what I fhou'd want,
  If I cou'd get but a man.
    Woo'd, and married, &c.

Wat ye wha I met Yeftreen?

NOW wat ye wha I met yeftreen,
    Coming down the ftreet, my jo?
My miftrefs in her tartan fcreen,
Fow bonny, braw, and fweet, my jo.
My dear, quoth I, thanks to the night,
That never wifh'd a lover ill,
Since ye're out of your mither's fight,
Let's take a wauk up to the hill.

  O KATY, wiltu' gang wi' me,
And leave the dinfome town a while?
The bloffom's fprouting frae the tree,
And a' the fimmer's gaw'n to fmile :
The mavis, nightingale, and lark,
The bleating lambs, and whiftling hind,
In ilka dale, green, fhaw, and park,
Will nourifh health, and glad ye'r mind.

  Soon as the clear goodman of day
Bends up his morning-draught of dew,
We'll gae to fome burn-fide and play,
And gather flowers to bufk ye'r brow :

We'll pou the daisies on the green,
The lucken gowans frae the bog;
Between hands now and then we'll lean,
And sport upo' the velvet fog.

There's up into a pleasant glen,
A wee piece frae my father's tow'r,
A canny, soft, and flow'ry den,
Where circling birks have form'd a bow'r:
Whene'er the sun grows high and warm,
We'll to the cauler shade remove;
There will I lock thee in mine arm,
And love and kiss, and kiss and love.

KATY's Answer.

MY mither's ay glowran o'er me,
　　Though she did the same before me;
I canna get leave to look to my loove,
　　Or else she'll be like to devour me.

Right fain wad I take ye'r offer,
　　Sweet Sir, but I'll tine my tocher;
Then, SANDY, ye'll fret, and wyte ye'r poor KATE,
　　Whene'er ye keek in your toom coffer.

For tho' my father has plenty
　　Of siller and plenishing dainty,
Yet he's unco swear to twin wi' his gear;
　　And sae we had need to be tenty.

Tutor my parents wi' caution,
　　Be wylie in ilka motion;
Brag weel o' ye'r land, and there's my leal hand,
　　Win them, I'll be at your devotion.

We'll a' to Kelfo go.

AN I'll awa' to bonny Tweed-fide,
 And fee my deary come throw,
And he fall be mine, gif fae he incline,
 For I hate to lead apes below.

While young and fair, I'll make it my care,
 To fecure myfell in a jo ;
I'm no fick a fool to let my blood cool,
 And fyne gae lead apes below.

Few words, bonny lad, will eithly perfuade,
 Though blufhing, I daftly fay, no ;
Gae on with your ftrain, and doubt not to gain,
 For I hate to lead apes below.

Unty'd to a man, do whate'er we can,
 We never can thrive or dow;
Then I will do well, do better wha will,
 And let them lead apes below.

Our time is precious, and gods are gracious,
 That beauties upon us beftow :
'Tis not to be thought we got them for nought,
 Or to be fet up for a fhow.

'Tis carried by votes, come, kilt up ye'r coats,
 And let us to Edinburgh go.
Where fhe that's bonny may catch a JOHNY,
 And never lead apes below.

Wayward Wife.

ALAS ! my fon, you little know,
    The forrows that from wedlock flow.
Farewell to every day of eafe,
When you've gotten a wife to pleafe :
   Sae bide you yet, and bide you yet,
   Ye little ken what's to betide you yet,
   The half of that will gane you yet,
   If a wayward wife obtain you yet.

The black cow on your foot ne'er trod,
Which gars you fing alang the road,
   Sae bide you yet, &c.

Sometimes the rock, fometimes the reel,
Or fome piece of the fpinning wheel,
She will drive at ye wi' good will,
And then fhe'll fend ye to the deil.
   Sae bide ye yet, &c.

When I like you was young and free,
I valu'd not the proudeft fhe ;
Like you I vainly boafted then,
That men alone were born to reign ;
   But bide you yet, &c.

Great HERCULES and SAMSON too,
Were ftronger men than I or you ;
Yet they were baffled by their dears,
And felt the diftaff and the fheers;
   Sae bide you yet, &c.

Stout gates of brafs, and well-built walls,
Are proof 'gainft fwords and cannon-balls,
But nought is found by fea or land,
That can a wayward wife withftand :
    Sae bide you yet, &c.

We're gayly yet.

W E'RE gayly yet, *and we're gayly yet,*
    And we're no very fou, but we're gayly yet ;
Then fit ye a while, and tipple a bit,
For we're no very fou, but we're gayly yet.
There was a lad and they ca'd him DICKY,
He gae me a kifs, and I bit his lippy ;
Then under my apron he fhew'd me a trick ;
And we're no very fou', but we're gayly yet.
    And we're gayly yet, &c.

There were three lads, and they were clad,
There were three laffes, and they them had,
Three trees in the orchard are newly fprung,
And we's a' get gear enough, we're but young,
    Then up wi't AILLIE, AILLIE,
      Up wi't, AILLIE, now,
    Then up wi't, AILLIE, quo' cummer,
    We's a' get roaring fou.

And one was kifs'd in the barn,
    Another was kifs'd on the green,
The third behind the peafe ftack,
    Till the mow flew up to her een.
    Then up wi't, &c.

Now, fy, JOHN THOMSON, rin,
    Gin ever ye ran in your life ;
De'il get you, but hey, my dear JACK,
    There's a man got a-bed with your wife.
     Then up wi't, &c.

Then away JOHN THOMSON ran,
    And I trow he ran with speed ;
But before he had run his length,
    The false loon had done the deed.
     We're gayly yet, &c.

Up and war them a', WILLIE.

WHEN we went to the field of war,
    And to the Weaponshaw, WILLIE,
With true design to stand our ground,
    And chace our faes awa', WILLIE ;
Lairds and Lords came there bedeen,
    And vow gin they were pra', WILLIE,
    Up and war 'em a', WILLIE,
    War 'em, war 'em a', WILLIE.

And when our army was drawn up,
    The brawest e'er I saw, WILLIE,
We did not doubt to rax the rout,
    And win the day and a', WILLIE.
Pipers play'd frae right to left,
    Fy, fourugh Whigs awa', WILLIE.
    Up and war, &c.

But when our standard was set up,
    So fierce the wind did pla', WILLIE,

The golden knop down from the top,
　　Unto the ground did fa', WILLIE.
Then fecond-fighted SANDY faid,
　　We'll do nae good at a', WILLIE.
　　Up and war, &c.

When bra'ly they attack'd our left,
　　Our front, and flank, and a', WILLIE;
Our bald commander on the green,
　　Our faes their left did ca', WILLIE,
And there the greateft flaughter made
　　That e'er poor TONALD faw, WILLIE.
　　Up and war, &c.

Firft when they faw our Highland mob,
　　They fwore they'd flay us a', WILLIE:
And yet ane fyl'd his breiks for fear,
　　And fo did rin awa', WILLIE.
We drave him back to-Bonnybrigs,
　　Dragoons, and foot, and a', WILLIE.
　　Up and war, &c.

But when their gen'ral view'd our lines,
　　And them in order faw, WILLIE,
He ftraight did march into the town,
　　And back his left did draw, WILLIE.
Thus we taught him the better gate
　　To get a better fa', WILLIE.
　　Up and war, &c.

And then we rally'd on the hills,
　　And bravely up did draw, WILLIE:
But gin ye fpear wha wan the day,
　　I'll tell you what I faw, WILLIE:

We baith did fight, and baith were beat,
  And baith did rin awa', WILLIE.
So there's my canty Highland fang
  About the thing I faw, WILLIE.

Up in the Air.

NOW the fun's gane out of fight,
  Beet the ingle, and fnuff the light.
In glens the fairies fkip and dance,
And witches wallop o'er to France.
  Up in the air, on my bonny grey mare,
And I fee her yet, and I fee her yet,
    Up in, &c.

The wind's drifting hail and fna',
O'er frozen hags, like a foot-ba';
Nae ftarns keek thro' the azure flit,
'Tis cauld and mirk as ony pit.
  The man i' the moon is caroufing aboon,
D' ye fee, d' ye fee, d' ye fee him yet?
    The man, &c.

Tak your glafs to clear your een,
'Tis the elixir heals the fpleen,
Baith wit and mirth it will infpire,
And gently puff the lover's fire:
  Up in the air, it drives awa' care;
Ha'e wi' ye, ha'e wi' ye, and ha'e wi' ye, lads, yet
    Up in, &c.

Steek the doors, had out the froft;
Come, WILLIE, gie's about ye'r toaft;

Till't lads, and lilt it out,
And let us hae a blythfome bout.
   Up wi't there, there, dinna cheat, but drink fair :
Huzza, huzza, and huzza, lads, yet.
   Up wi't, &c.

The yellow-hair'd Laddie.

THE yellow-hair'd laddie fat down on yon brae,
   Cries, Milk the ewes, laffie, let nane of them gae;
And ay fhe milked, and ay fhe fang,
The yellow-hair'd laddie fhall be my goodman.
   And ay fhe milked, &c.

The weather is cauld, and my claithing is thin,
The ewes are new clipped, they winna bught in;
They winna bught in tho' I fhou'd die,
O yellow-hair'd laddie, be kind to me,
   They winna bught in, &c.

The goodwife cries butt the houfe, JENNY, come ben;
The cheefe is to mak, and the butter's to kirn;
Tho' butter, and cheefe, and a' fhou'd fowre,
I'll crack and kifs wi' my love ae haff hour ;
It's ae haff hour, and we's e'en mak it three,
For the yellow-hair'd laddie my hufband fhall be.

The Wife of Auchtermuchty.

IN Auchtermuchty dwelt a man,
   An hufband, as I heard it tawld,
Quha weil coud tipple out a can,
   And nowther luvit hungir nor cauld;

L 3

Till anes it fell upon a day,
   He zokit his plewch upon the plain;
And fchort the ftorm wald let him ftay,
   Sair blew the day with wind and rain.

He loofd the plewch at the lands end,
   And draife his owfen hame at ene;
Quhen he came in he blinkit ben,
   And faw his Wyfe baith dry and clene,
Set beikand by a fyre fu' bauld,
   Suppand fat fowp, as I heard fay:
The man being weary, wet, and cauld,
   Betwein thir twa it was nae play.

Quod he, Quhair is my horfes corn,
   My owfen has nae hay nor ftrae,
Dame, ze maun to the plewch the morn,
   I fall be hufiy gif I may.
This feid-time it proves cauld and bad,
   And ze fit warm, nae troubles fe;
The morn ze fall gae wi' the lad,
   And fyne zeil ken what drinkers drie.

Gudeman, quod fcho, content am I,
   To tak the plewch my day about,
Sae ye rule weil the kaves and ky,
   And all the houfe baith in and out:
And now fen ze baif made the law,
   Then gyde all richt and do not break;
They ficker raid that neir did faw,
   Therefore let naething be neglect.

But fen ye will huffyfkep ken,
   Firft ze maun fift and fyne fall kned;
And ay as ze gang butt and ben,
   Luke that the bairns dryt not the bed;

And lay a faft wyfp to the kiln,
   We haif a dear farm on our heid ;
And ay as ze gang forth and in,
   Keip weil the gaiflings frae the gled.

The wyfe was up richt late at ene,
   I pray luck gife her ill to fair,
Scho kirn'd the kirn, and fkumt it clene,
   Left the gudeman but bledoch bair :
Then in the morning up fcho gat ;
   And on her heart laid her disjune,
And pat as mickle in her lap,
   As micht haif ferd them baith at nune.

Says, Jok, be thou maifter of wark,
   And thou fall had, and I fall ka,
Ife promife thee a gude new fark,
   Either of round claith or of fma.
She lowft the oufen aught or nyne,
   And hynt a gad-ftaff in her hand ;
Up the Gudeman raife aftir fyne,
   And faw the Wyfe had done command.

He draif the gaiflings forth to feid,
   Thair was but fevenfum of them aw,
And by thair comes the greidy gled,
   And lickt up fiye, left him but twa :
Then out he rane in all his mane,
   How fune he hard the gaifling cry ;
But than or he came in again,
   The kaves brake loufe and fuckt the ky.

The caves and ky met in the loan,
   The man ran wi' a rung to red,
Than by came an illwilly roan,
   And brodit his buttocks till they bled.

Syne up he tuke a rok of tow,
    And he fat down to fey the fpinning;
He loutit doun our neir the low,
    Quod he, This wark has ill beginning.

The leam up throu the lum did flow,
    The fute tuke fire, it flyed him than;
Sum lumps did fa' and burn his pow;
    I wat he was a dirty man;
Zit he gat water in a pan,
    Quherwith he flokend out the fyre:
To foup the houfe he fyne began,
    To had all richt was his defyre.

Hyrd to the kirn then did he ftoure;
    And jumblit at it till he fwat,
Quhen he had rumblit a full lang hour,
    The forrow crap of butter he gat;
Albeit nae butter he could get,
    Zet he was cummert wi' the kirn,
And fyne he het the milk fae het,
    That ill a fpark of it wad zyrne.

Then ben thair came a greedy fow,
    I trow he cund her little thank:
For in fcho fhot her mickle mow,
    And ay fcho winkit, and ay fcho drank;
He tuke the kirnftaff be the fchank,
    And thocht to reik the fow a root,
The twa left gaiflings gat a clank,
    That ftraik dang baith their harns out.

Then he bure kendling to the kill,
    But fcho ftart up all in a low,
Quhat eir he heard, what eir he faw,
    That day he had nae will to **.

Then he zied to tak up the bairns,
  Thocht to have fund them fair and clene,
The firſt that he gat in his arms,
  Was a bedirtin to the ene.

The firſt it ſmellt ſae ſappylie,
  To touch the lave he did not grien:
The deil cut aff thair hands, quoth he,
  That cramd zour kytes ſae ſtrute zeſtrein.
He traild the foul ſheits down the gate,
  Thocht to have waſht them on a ſtane,
The burn was riſen grit of ſpait,
  Away frae him the ſheits has tane.

Then up he gat on a know-heid,
  On hir to cry, on hir to ſhout;
Scho hard him, and ſcho hard him not,
  But ſtoutly ſteird the ſtots about.
Scho draif the day unto the nicht,
  Scho lowſt the plewch, and ſyne came hame;
Scho fand all wrang that ſould bene richt,
  I trow the man thocht mekle ſchame.

Quoth he, My office I forſake,
  For all the hale days of my lyfe;
For I wald put a houſe to wraik,
  Had I been twenty days gudewyfe.
Quoth ſcho, Weil mot ze bruik your place,
  For truly I ſall neir accept it;
Quoth he, Feynd fa the lyar's face,
  But zit ze may be blyth to get it.

Then up ſcho gat a meikle rung;
  And the gudeman made to the dore,
Quoth he, Dame, I ſall hald my tung,
  For an we fecht I'll get the war.

Quoth he, When I forfuke my plewch,
　I trow I, but forfuke my fkill:
Then I will to my plewch again;
　For I and this houfe will nevir do weil.

Bannocks of Barley-meal.

MY name is ARGYLL: you may think it ftrange,
　　To live at the court, and never to change;
All falfehood and flatt'ry I do difdain;
In my fecret thoughts no deceit fhall remain:
In fiege or in battle I ne'er was difgrac'd;
I always my king and my country have fac'd;
I'll do any thing for my country's well,
I'd live upo' bannocks o' barley-meal.

Adieu to the courtiers of London town,
For to my ain country I will gang down;
At the fight of Kirkaldy ance again,
I'll cock up my bonnet, and march amain.
O the muckle de'il tak a' your noife and ftrife,
I'm fully refolv'd for a country life,
Where a' the bra' laffes, wha kens me well,
Will feed me wi' bannocks o' barley-meal.

　I'll quickly lay down my fword and my gun,
And I'll put my plaid and my bonnet on,
Wi' my plaiding ftockings and leather-heel'd fhoon;
They'll mak me appear a fine fprightly loon.
And when I am dreft thus frae tap to tae,
Hame to my MAGGIE I think for to gae,
Wi' my claymore hinging down to my heel,
To whang at the bannocks o' barley-meal.

I'll buy a fine prefent to bring to my dear,
A pair of fine garters for MAGGIE to wear,
And fome pretty things elfe, I do declare,
When fhe gangs wi' me to Paifley fair.
And whan we are married we'll keep a cow,
My MAGGIE fall milk her, and I will plow :
We'll live a' the winter on beef and lang-kail,
And whang at the bannocks of barley-meal.

If my MAGGIE fhou'd chance to bring me a fon,
He's fight for his king, as his daddy has done ;
I'll fend him to Flanders fome breeding to learn,
Syne hame into Scotland and keep a farm.
And thus we'll live and induftrious be,
And wha'll be fae great as my MAGGIE and me ;
We'll foon grow as fat as a Norway feal,
Wi' feeding on bannocks o' barley-meal.

Adieu to you citizens every ane,
Wha jolt in your coaches to Drury-lane ;
You bites of Bear-garden who fight for gains,
And you fops who have got more wigs than brains ;
You cullies and bullies, I'll bid you adieu,
For whoring and fwearing I'll leave it to you ;
Your woodcock and pheafant, your duck and your teal,
I'll leave them for bannocks o' barley-meal.

I'll leave aff kiffing a citizen's wife,
I'm fully refolv'd for a country life ;
Kiffing and toying, I'll fpend the lang day,
Wi' bonny young laffes on cocks of hay ;
Where each clever lad gives his bonny lafs
A kifs and a tumble upo' the green grafs.
I'll awa' to the Highlands as faft's I can reel,
And whang at the bannocks o' barley-meal.

No Dominies for me, laddie.

I CHANC'D to meet an airy blade,
　　A new-made pulpiteer, laddie,
With cock'd-up hat and powder'd wig,
　　Black coat and cuffs fu' clear, laddie;
A long cravat at him did wag,
　　And buckles at his knee, laddie;
Says he, My heart, by CUPID's dart, ·
　　Is captivate to thee, laffie.

I'll rather chufe to thole grim death;
　　So ceafe and let me be, laddie:
For what? fays he; Good troth, faid I,
　　No dominies for me, laddie.　　　　　.
Minifters' ftipends are uncertain rents
　　For ladies' conjunct-fee, laddie;
When books and gowns are all cried down,
　　No dominies for me, laddie.

But for your fake I'll fleece the flock,
　　Grow rich as I grow auld, laffie;
If I be fpar'd I'll be a laird,
　　And thou's be Madam call'd, laffie.
But what if ye fhou'd chance to die,
　　Leave bairns, ane or twa, laddie?
Naething wad be referv'd for them
　　But hair-moul'd books to gnaw, laddie.

At this he angry was, I wat,
　　He gloom'd and look'd fu' high, laddie:
When I perceived this, in hafte
　　I left my dominie, laddie.

Fare ye well, my charming maid,
　　This leſſon learn of me, laſſie,
At the next offer hold him faſt,
　　That firſt makes love to thee, laſſie.

Then I returning hame again,
　　And coming down the town, laddie,
By my good luck I chanc'd to meet
　　A gentleman dragoon, laddie ;
And he took me by baith the hands,
　　'Twas help in time of need, laddie.
'Fools on ceremonies ſtand,
　　At twa words we agreed, laddie.

He led me to his quarter-houſe,
　　Where we exchang'd a word, laddie :
We had nae uſe for black-gowns there,
　　We married o'er the ſword, laddie.
Martial drums is muſic fine,
　　Compar'd wi' tinkling bells, laddie ;
Gold, red and blue, is more divine
　　Than black, the hue of hell, laddie.

Kings, queens, and princes, crave the aid
　　Of my brave ſtout dragoon, laddie ;
While dominies are much employ'd
　　'Bout whores and ſackloth gowns, laddie.
Away wi' a' theſe whining loons ;
　　They look like, Let me be, laddie :
I've more delight in roaring guns ;
　　No dominies for me, laddie.

JAMIE gay.

AS JAMIE gay gang'd blyth his way
    Along the river Tweed,
A bonny lafs as e'er was feen,
    Came tripping o'er the mead.
The hearty fwain, untaught to feign,
    The buxom nymph furvey'd,
And full of glee as lad could be,
    Befpoke the pretty maid.

Dear Laffie tell, why by thinefell
    Thou haft'ly wand'reft here.
My ewes, fhe cry'd, are ftraying wide,
    Canft tell me, laddie, where?
To town I'll hie, he made reply,
    Some meikle fport to fee,
But thou'rt fo fweet, fo trim and neat,
    I'll feek the ewes with thee.

She gi'm her hand, nor made a ftand,
    But lik'd the youth's intent;
O'er hill and dale, o'er plain and vale
    Right merrily they went.
The birds fang fweet, the pair to greet,
    And flowers bloom'd around?
And as they walk'd, of love they talk'd,
    And joys which lovers crown'd.

And now the fun had rofe to noon,
    The zenith of his power,
When to a fhade their fteps they made,
    To pafs the mid-day hour.

The bonny lad rowd in his plaid
  The lafs, who fcorn'd to frown;
She foon forgot the ewes fhe fought,
  And he to gang to town.

I've been Courting.

I'VE been-courting at a lafs
  Thefe twenty days and mair;
Her father winna gi'e me her,
  She has fick a gleib of gear.
But gin I had her where I wou'd
  Amang the hether here,
I'd ftrive to win her kindnefs,
  For a' her father's care.

For fhe's a bonny fonfy lafs,
  An armsfu', I fwear;
I wou'd marry her without a coat,
  Or e'er a plack o' gear.
For, truft me, when I faw her firft,
  She gae me fick a wound,
That a' the doctors i' the earth
  Can never mak me found.

For when fhe's abfent frae my fight,
  I think upon her ftill;
And when I fleep, or when I wake,
  She does my fenfes fill.

M 2

May Heavens guard the bonny laſs
　That ſweetens a' my life;
And ſhame fa' me gin e'er I ſeek
　Anither for my wife.

My Heart's my ain.

'TIS nae very lang ſinſyne,
　That I had a lad of my ain;
But now he's awa' to anither,
　And left me a' my lain.
The laſs he's courting has ſiller,
　And I hae nane at a';
And 'tis nought but the love of the tocher
　That's tane my lad awa'.

But I'm blyth, that my heart's my ain,
　And I'll keep it a' my life,
Until that I meet wi' a lad
　Who has ſenſe to wale a good wife.
For though I ſay't myſell,
　That ſhou'd nae ſay't, 'tis true,
The lad that gets me for a wife,
　He'll ne'er hae occaſion to rue.

I gang ay fou clean and fou toſh,
　As a' the neighbours can tell;
Though I've ſeldom a gown on my back,
　But ſick as I ſpin myſell.
And when I am clad in my curtſey,
　I think myſell as braw
As S⸲⸲⸲⸲, wi' a' her pearling
　That's tane my lad awa'.

But I wiſh they were buckled together,
  And may they live happy for life ;
Tho' WILLIE does-flight me, and's left me,
  The chield he deſerves a good wife.
But, O ! I'm blyth that I've miſs'd him,
  As blyth as I weel can be ;
For ane that's ſae keen o' the ſiller
  Will ne'er agree wi' me.

But as the truth is, I'm hearty,
  I hate to be ſcrimpit or ſcant ;
The wie thing I hae, I'll make uſe o't,
  And nae ane about me ſhall want.
For I'm a good guide o' the warld,
  I ken when to ha'd and to gie ;
For whinging and cringing for ſiller
  Will ne'er agree wi' me.

Contentment is better than riches,
  An' he wha has that has enough ;
The maſter is ſeldom ſae happy
  As ROBIN that drives the plough.
But if a young lad wou'd caſt up,
  To make me his partner for life ;
If the chield has the ſenſe to be happy,
  He'll fa' on his feet for a wife.

My Wife's ta'en the Gee.

A FRIEND of mine came here yeſtreen,
    And he wou'd hae me down
To drink a bottle of ale wi' him
    In the nieſt borrows town.

But, O! indeed, it was, Sir,
  Sae far the war for me ;
For lang or e'er that I came hame,
  My wife had ta'en the gee.

We fat fae late, and drank fae ftout,
  The truth I tell to you,
That lang or e'er midnight came,
  We were a' roaring fou.
My wife fits at the fire-fide ;
  And the tear blinds ay her ee,
The ne'er a bed will fhe gae to;
  But fit and tak the gee.

In the morning foon, when I came down,
  The ne'er a word fhe fpake ;
But mony a fad and four look,
  And ay her head fhe'd fhake.
My dear, quoth I, what aileth thee,
  To look fae four on me ?
I'll never do the like again,
  If you'll never tak the gee.

When that fhe heard, fhe ran, fhe flang
  Her arms about my neck ;
And twenty kiffes in a crack,
  And, poor wee thing, fhe grat.
If you'll ne'er do the like again,
  But bide at hame wi' me,
I'll lay my life Ife be the wife
  That's never tak the gee.

Wallifou fa' the Cat.

THERE was a bonnie wi' laddie,
   Was keeping a bonny whine fheep;
There was a bonnie wee laffie,
   Was wading the water fae deep,.
Was wading the water fae deep,
   And a little above her knee;
The laddie cries unto the laffie,
   Come down Tweedfide to me.

And when I gade down Tweed-fide,
   I heard, I dinna ken what,
I heard ae wife fay t' anither,
   Wallifou fa' the cat;
Wallifou fa' the cat,
   She's bred the houfe an wan eafe,
She's open'd the am'ry door,
   And eaten up a' the cheefe.

She's eaten up a' the cheefe,
   O' the kebbuk fhe's no left a bit;
She's dung down the bit fkate on the braze,
   And 'tis fa'en in the fowen kit;
'Tis out o' the fowen kit,
   And 'tis into the maifter-can;
It will be fae fiery fa't,
   'Twill poifon our goodman,

Here awa', there awa'.

HERE awa', there awa', here awa' WILLIE,
    Here awa', there awa', here awa' hame;
Lang have I fought thee, dear have I bought thee;
    Now I have gotten my WILLIE again.

Thro' the lang muir I have follow'd my WILLIE,
Thro' the lang muir I have follow'd him hame,
Whatever betide us, nought fhall divide us;
Love now rewards all my forrow and pain.

Here awa', there awa', here awa', WILLIE,
Here awa', there awa', here awa' hame,
Come Love, believe me, nothing can grieve me,
Ilka thing pleafes while WILLIE's at hame.

Drap of Capie----O.

THERE liv'd a wife in our gate-end,
    She lo'ed a drap of capie--O,
And all the gear that e'er fhe gat,
    She flipt it in her gabie---O.

Upon a frofty winter's night,
    The wife had got a drapie--O,
And fhe had pifh'd her coats fae weil,
    She could not find the patie---O.

But fhe's awa' to her goodman,
    They ca'd him TAMIE LAMIE--O,
Gae ben and fetch the cave to me,
    That I may get a dramie---O.

TAMIE was an honeſt man,
 Himſelf he took a drapie---O,
It was nae weil out o'er his craig,
 Till ſhe was on his tapie---O.

She paid him weil, baith back and ſide,
 And ſair ſhe creiſh'd his backie---O,
And made his ſkin baith blue and black,
 And gar'd his ſhoulders crackie---O.

Then he's awa' to the malt barn,
 And he has ta'en a pockie---O,
He put her in, baith head and tail,
 And caſt her o'er his backie---O.

The carling ſpurn'd wi' head and feet,
 The carle he was ſae ackie---O,
To ilka wall that he came by,
 He gar'd her head play knackie---O.

Goodman, I think you'll murder me,
 My brains you out will knockie---O,
He gi'd her ay the other hitch,
 Lie ſtill, you devil's buckie---O.

Goodman, I'm like to make my burn,
 O let me out, good TAMIE---O;
Then he ſet her upon a ſtane,
 And bade her piſh a damie---O.

Then TAMIE took her aff the ſtane,
 And put her in the pockie---O,
And when ſhe did begin to ſpurn,
 He lent her ay a knockie---O.

Away he went to the mill-dam,
 And there ga'e her a duckie---O,

And ilka chiel that had a ſtick,
   Play'd thump upon her backie---O.

And when he took her hame again,
   He did hing up the pockie---O,
At her bed-ſide, as I hear ſay,
   Upon a little knagie---O.

And ilka day that ſhe up-roſe,
   In naithing but her ſmockie---O,
Sae ſoon as ſhe look'd o'er the bed,
   She might behold the pockie---O.

Now all ye men, baith far and near,
   That have a drunken tutie---O,
Duck you your wives in time of year,
   And I'll lend you the pockie---O,

The wife did live for nineteen years,
   And was fu' frank and cuthie---O,
And ever ſince ſhe got the duck,
   She never had the drouthie---O.

At laſt the carling chanc'd to die,
   And TAMIE did her bury---O,
And for the publick benefit,
   He has gar'd print the curie---O.

And this he did her motto make ;
   Here lies an honeſt luckie---O,
Who never left the drinking trade,
   Until ſhe got a duckie---O.

MY daddy left me gear enough,
   A couter, and an auld beam-plough,
A nebbed ſtaff, a nutting-tyne,
A' fiſhing wand with hook and line;
With twa auld ſtools, and a dirt-houſe,
A jerkenet ſcarce worth a louſe,
An auld patt, that wants the lug,
A ſpurtle and a ſowen mug.

A hempken heckle, and a mell,
A tar-horn, and a weather's bell,
A muck-fork, and an auld peet-creel,
The ſpakes of our auld ſpinning-wheel.
A pair of branks, yea, and a ſaddle,
With our auld brunt and broken laddle,
A whang-bit, and a ſniſſle-bit;
Chear up, my bairns, and dance a fit.

A flailing-ſtaff and a timmer ſpit,
An auld kirn and a hole in it,
Yarn-winnles, and a reel,
A fetter-lock, a trump of ſteel,
A whiſtle, and a tup-horn ſpoon,
With an auld pair of clouted ſhoon,
A timmer ſpade, and a gleg ſhear,
A bonnet for my bairns to wear.

A timmer tong, a broken cradle,
The pillion of an auld car-ſaddle,
A gullie-knife, and a horſe-wand,
A mitten for the left hand,

With an auld broken pan of brafs,
With an auld fark that wants the arfe,
An auld-band, and a hoodling how,
I hope, my bairns, ye're a weil now.

Aft have I borne ye on my back,
With a' this riff-raff in my pack;
And it was a' for want of gear,
That gart me fteal Mefs Jo h n's grey mare:
But now, my bairns, what ails ye now?
For ye ha'e naigs enough to plow;
And hofe and fhoon fit for your feet,
Chear up, my bairns, and dinna greet.

Then with myfel I did advife,
My daddy's gear for to comprize;
Some neighbours I ca'd in to fee
What gear my daddy left to me.
They fat three quarters of a year,
Comprizing of my daddy's gear;
And when they had gi'en a' their votes,
'Twas fcarcely a' worth four pounds Scots.

The Ploughman.

THE ploughman he's a bonny lad,
  And a' his wark's at leifure,
And when that he comes hame at ev'n,
  He kiffes me wi' pleafure.
    Up wi't now, my ploughman lad,
    Up wi't now, my ploughman;
    Of a' the lads that I do fee,
    Commend me to the ploughman.

Now the blooming fpring comes on,
 He takes his yoking early,
And whiftling o'er the furrow'd land,
 He goes to fallow clearly ;
  Up wi't now, &c.

Whan my ploughman comes hame at ev'n,
 He's often wet and weary ;
Caft aff the wet, put on the dry,
 And gae to bed, my deary.
  Up wi't now, &c.

I will wafh my ploughman's hofe,
 And I will wafh his o'erlay,
And I will make my ploughman's bed,
 And chear him late and early.
  Merry butt, and merry ben,
  Merry is my ploughman ;
  Of a' the trades that I do ken,
  Commend me to the ploughman.

Plough you hill, and plough you dale,
 Plough you faugh and fallow,
Who winna drink the ploughman's health,
 Is but a dirty fellow.
  Merry butt, and, &c.

The Tailor.

THE tailor came to clout the claife,
 Sick a braw fellow,
He fill'd the houfe a' fou of fleas,
 Daffin down, and daffin down,

Vol. II.   N

He fill'd the houfe a' fou of fleas,
 Daffin down and dilly.

The laffie flept ayont the fire,
 Sic a braw hiffey !
Oh ! fhe was a' his heart's defire ;
 Daffin down, and daffin down ;
Oh ! fhe was a' his heart's defire :
 Daffin down and dilly.

The laffie fhe fell faft afleep ;
 Sic a braw hiffey !
The tailor clofe to her did creep ;
 Daffin down, and daffin down ;
The tailor clofe to her did creep ;
 Daffin down and dilly.

The laffie waken'd in a fright ;
 Sic a braw hiffey !
Her maidenhead had taen the flight ;
 Daffin down, and daffin down ;
Her maidenhead had taen the flight ;
 Daffin down and dilly.

She fought it butt, fhe fought it ben ;
 Sic a braw hiffey !
And in beneath the clocken-hen ;
 Daffin down, and daffin down ;
And in beneath the clocken-hen ;
 Daffin down and dilly.

She fought it in the owfen-ftaw ;
 Sic a braw hiffey !
No, faith, quo' fhe, it's quite awa' ;
 Daffin down, and daffin down,

Na, faith, quo' she, it's quite awa';
   Daffin down and dilly.

She fought it 'yont the knocking stane;
   Sic a braw hissey!
Some day, quo' she, 'twill gang its lane;
   Daffin down, and daffin down;
Some day, quo' she, 'twill gang its lane;
   Daffin down and dilly.

She ca'd the taylor to the court;
   Sic a braw hissey!
And a' the young men round about;
   Daffin down, and daffin down:
And a' the young men round about;
   Daffin down and dilly.

She gard the tailor pay a fine;
   Sic a braw hissey!
Gie me my maidenhead agen;
   Daffin down, and daffin down;
Gie me my maidenhead agen;
   Daffin down and dilly.

O what way wad ye hae't agen?
   Sic a braw hissey!
Oh! just the way that it was taen;
   Daffin down, and daffin down;
Oh! just the way that it was taen;
   Daffin down and dilly.

N 2

The maid gaed to the Mill.

THE maid's gane to the mill by night,
   Hech hey, fae wanton;
The maid's gane to the mill by night,
   Hey fae wanton fhe;
She's fworn by moon and ftars fae bright,
That fhe fhould hae her corn ground,
That fhe fhould hae her corn ground,
   Mill and multure free.

Out then came the miller's man,
   Hech hey, fae wanton;
Out then came the miller's man,
   Hey fae wanton he;
He fware he'd do the beft he can,
For to get her corn ground,
For to get her corn ground,
   Mill and multure free.

He put his hand about her neck,
   Hech hey, fae wanton;
He put his hand about her neck,
   Hey fae wanton he;
He dang her down upon a fack,
And there fhe got her corn ground,
And there fhe got her corn ground,
   Mill and multure free.

When other maids gaed out to play,
   Hech hey, fae wanton;
When other maids gaed out to play,
   Hey fae wantonlie;

She figh'd and fobb'd, and wadnae ftay,
Becaufe fhe'd got her corn ground,
Becaufe fhe'd got her corn ground,
   Mill and multure free.

When forty weeks were paft and gane,
   Hech hey, fae wanton :
When forty weeks were paft and gane,
   Hey fae wantonlie ;
This maiden had a braw lad-bairn,
Becaufe fhe'd got her corn ground,
Becaufe fhe'd got her corn ground,
   Mill and multure free.

Her mither bade her caft it out,
   - Hech hey, fae wanton ;
Her mither bade her caft it out,
   Hey fae wantonlie ;
It was the miller's dufty clout,
For getting of her corn ground,
For getting of her corn ground,
   Mill and multure free.

Her father bade her keep it in,
   Hech hey, fae wanton ;
Her father bade her keep it in,
   Hey fae wantonlie,
It was the chief of a' her kin,
Becaufe fhe'd got her corn ground,
Becaufe fhe'd got her corn ground,
   Mill and multure free.

The brisk young Lad.

THERE came a young man to my daddie's door,
  My daddie's door, my daddie's door,
There came a young man to my daddie's door,
    Came seeking me to woo.
  And wow but he was a braw young lad,
  A brisk young lad, and a braw young lad,
  And wow but he was a braw young lad,
    Came seeking me to woo.

But I was baking when he came,
When he came, when he came ;
I took him in and gae him a scone,
    To thow his frozen mou'.
    And wow but, &c.

I set him in aside the bink,
I gae him bread, and ale to drink,
And ne'er a blyth styme wad he blink,
    Until his wame was fou.
    And wow but, &c.

Gae, get ye gone, ye cauldrife wooer,
Ye sour-looking, cauldrife wooer,
I straightway show'd him to the door,
    Saying, Come nae mair to woo.
    And wow but, &c.

There lay a duck-dub before the door,
Before the door, before the door,
There lay a duck-dub before the door,
    And there fell he I trow.
    And wow but, &c.

Out came the goodman, and high he shouted,
Out came the goodwife, and low she louted,
And a' the town-neighbours were gather'd about it,
    And there lay he I trow.
     And wow but, &c.

Then out came I, and sneer'd and smil'd,
Ye came to woo, but ye're a' beguil'd,
Ye'ave fa'en i' the dirt, and ye're a befyl'd.
    We'll hae nae mair of you.
     And wow but, &c.

The Surprise.

I HAD a horse, and I had nae mair,
    I gat him frae my daddy ;
My purse was light, and my heart was sair,
    But my wit it was fu' ready.
And sae I thought upon a wile,
    Outwittens of my daddy,
To fee myself to a lowland laird,
    Who had a bonny lady.

I wrote a letter, and thus began,
    Madam, be not offended,
I'm o'er the lugs in love wi' you,
    And care not tho' ye kend it.
For I get little frae the laird,
    And far less frae my daddy,
And I would blythly be the man
    Would strive to please my lady.

She read my letter, and she leuch,
   Ye needna been sae blate, man ;
You might hae come to me yoursell,
   And tald me o' your state, man :
You might hae come to me yoursell,
   Outwittens of your daddy,
And made JOHN GOUCKSTON of the laird,
   And kiss'd his bonny lady.

Then she pat siller in my purse,
   We drank wine in a cogie ;
She fee'd a man to rub my horse,
   And wow but I was vogie :
But I gat ne'er sae fair a fleg
   Since I came frae my daddy,
The laird came rap rap to the yate,
   Whan I was wi' his lady.

Then she pat me below a chair,
   And hap'd me wi' a plaidie ;
But I was like to swarf wi' fear,
   And wish'd me wi' my daddy.
The laird went out, he saw na me,
   I went whan I was ready :
I promis'd, but I ne'er gade back
   To see his bonny lady.

The Mariner's Wife.

BUT are you sure the news is true?
   And are you sure he's weel?
Is this a time to think o' wark?
   Ye jades, fling by your wheel.

There's nae luck about the house,
 There's nae luck at a',
There's nae luck about the house
 When our goodman's awa'.

Is this a time to think of wark,
 When Colin's at the door?
Rax me my cloak, I'll down the key,
 And fee him come afhore.
  There's nae luck, &c.

Rife up, and mak a clean fire-fide,
 Put on the muckle pat;
Gie little Kate her cotton gown,
 And Jock his Sunday's coat.
  There's nae luck, &c.

Mak their fhoon as black as flaes,
 Their ftockings white as fnaw;
It's a' to pleafure our goodman,
 He likes to fee them braw.
  There's nae luck, &c.

There are twa hens into the crib,
 Have fed this month and mair,
Make hafte and thraw their necks about,
 That Colin weil may fare.
  There's nae luck, &c.

Bring down to me my bigonet,
 My bifhop-fattin gown,
And then gae tell the Bailie's wife,
 That Colin's come to town.
  There's nae luck, &c.

My Turkey flippers I'll put on,
  My ftockings pearl blue,
And a' to pleafure our goodman,
  For he's baith leel and true.
    There's nae luck, &c.

Sae fweet his voice, fae fmooth his tongue,
  His breath's like cauler air,
His very tread has mufic in't
  As he comes up the ftair.
    There's nae luck, &c.

And will I fee his face again,
  And will I hear him fpeak?
I'm downright dizzy with the joy,
  In troth I'm like to greet!
    There's nae luck, &c.

The Gawkie.

B LYTH young BESS to JEAN did fay,
  Will ye gang to yon funny brae,
Where flocks do feed, and herds do ftray,
  And fport a while wi' JAMIE?
Ah na, lafs, I'll no gang there,
  Nor about JAMIE tak nae care,
  Nor about JAMIE tak nae care;
For he's ta'en up wi' MAGGIE.

For hark, and I will tell you, lafs,
Did I not fee your JAMIE pafs,

Wi' muckle gladnefs in his face,
    Out o'er the muir to MAGGIE.
I wat he gae her mony a kifs,
And MAGGIE took them ne'er amifs ;
'Tween ilka fmack pleas'd her wi' this,
    That BESS was but a gawkie.

For whenever a civil kifs I feek,
She turns her head, and thraws her cheek,
And for an hour fhe'll fcarcely fpeak ;
    Who'd not ca' her a gawkie ?
But fure my MAGGIE has mair fenfe,
She'll gie a fcore without offence :
Now gi'e me ane unto the menfe,
    And ye fhall be my dawtie.

O JAMIE, ye hae mony tane,
But I will never ftand for ane
Or twa, when we do meet again,
    Sae ne'er think me a gawkie.
Ah na, lafs, that can ne'er be,
Sick thoughts as thefe are far frae me,
Or ony thy fweet face that fee,
    E'er to think thee a gawkie.

But, whifh't, nae mair of this we'll fpeak,
For yonder JAMIE does us meet ;
Inftead of MEG he kifs'd fae fweet,
    I trow he likes the gawkie.
O dear BESS, I hardly knew,
When I came by, your gown's fae new,
I think you've got it wat wi' dew.
    Quoth fhe, That's like a gawkie.

It's wat wi' dew, and 'twill get rain,
And I'll get gowns when it is gane,
Sae ye may gang the gate you came,
   And tell it to your dawtie.
The guilt appear'd in JAMIE's cheek,
He cry'd, O cruel maid, but fweet,
If I fhould gang another gate,
   I ne'er could meet my dawtie.

The laffes faft frae him they flew,
And left poor JAMIE fair to rue,
That ever MAGGIE's face he knew,
   Or yet ca'd BESS a gawkie.
As they gade o'er the muir they fang,
The hills and dales with echoes rang,
The hills and dales with echoes rang,
   Gang o'er the muir to MAGGIE.

The Shepherd's Son.

THERE was a fhepherd's fon,
   Kept fheep upon a hill,
He laid his pipe and crook afide,
   And there he flept his fill.
    Sing, Fal deral, &c.

He looked eaft, he looked weft,
   Then gave an under-look,
And there he fpied a lady fair,
   Swimming in a brook,
    Sing, Fal deral, &c.

He rais'd his head frae his green bed,
    And then approach'd the maid,
Put on your claiths, my dear, he fays,
    And be ye not afraid.
      Sing, Fal deral, &c.

'Tis fitter for a lady fair,
    To few her filken feam,
Than to get up in a May morning,
    And ftrive againft the ftream.
      Sing, Fal deral, &c.

If you'll not touch my mantle,
    And let my claiths alane ;
Then I'll give you as much money,
    As you can carry hame.
      Sing, Fal deral, &c.

O ! I'll not touch your mantle,
    And I'll let your claiths alane ;
But I'll tak you out of the clear water,
    My dear, to be my ain,
      Sing, Fal deral, &c.

And when fhe out of the water came,
    He took her in his arms;
Put on your claiths, my dear, he fays,
    And hide thofe lovely charms.
      Sing, Fal deral, &c.

He mounted her on a milk-white fteed,
    Himfelf upon anither ;
And all along the way they rode,
    Like fifter and like brither.
      Sing, Fal deral, &c.

VOL. II.   O

When fhe came to her father's yate,
  She tirled at the pin;
And ready ftood the porter there,
  To let this fair maid in.
    Sing, Fal deral, &c.

And when the gate was opened,
  So nimbly's fhe whipt in;
Pough! you're a fool without, fhe fays,
  And I'm a maid within.
    Sing, Fal deral, &c.

Then fare ye well, my modeft boy,
  I thank you for your care;
But had you done what you fhould do,
  I ne'er had left you there.
    Sing, Fal deral, &c.

Oh! I'll caft aff my hofe and fhoon,
  And let my feet gae bare,
And gin I meet a bonny lafs,
  Hang me, if her I fpare.
    Sing, Fal deral, &c.

In that do as you pleafe, fhe fays,
  But you fhall never more
Have the fame opportunity;
  With that fhe fhut the door.
    Sing, Fal deral, &c.

There is a gude auld proverb,
  I've often heard it told,
He that would not when he might,
  He fhould not when he would.
    Sing, Fal deral, &c.

Get up and bar the Door.

IT fell about the Martinmas time,
  And a gay time it was then,
When our goodwife got puddings to make,
  And fhe's boil'd them in the pan.

The wind fae cauld blew fouth and north,
  And blew into the floor:
Quoth our goodman, to our goodwife,
  " Gae out and bar the door."

" My hand is in my huffy'f fkap,
  Goodman, as ye may fee,
An it fhou'd nae be barr'd this hundred year,
  Its no be barr'd for me."

They made a paction 'tween them twa,
  They made it firm and fure;
That the firft word whae'er fhou'd fpeak,
  Shou'd rife and bar the door.

Then by there came two gentlemen,
  At twelve o'clock at night,
And they could neither fee houfe nor hall,
  Nor coal nor candle light.

Now, whether is this a rich man's houfe,
  Or whether is it a poor?
But never a word wad ane o' them fpeak,
  For barring of the door.

And firft they ate the white puddings,
  And then they ate the black;

Though muckle thought the goodwife to herfel,
　Yet ne'er a word fhe fpake.

Then faid the one unto the other,
　" Here, man, tak ye my knife,
Do ye tak aff the auld man's beard,
　And I'll kifs the goodwife."

" But there's nae water in the houfe,
　And what fhall we do than ?"
" What ails ye at the pudding broo,
　That boils into the pan ?"

O up then ftarted our goodman,
　An angry man was he ;
" Will ye kifs my wife before my een,
　And fcald me wi' pudding bree ?"

Then up and ftarted our goodwife,
　Gied three fkips on the floor ;
" Goodman, you've fpoken the foremoft word,
　Get up and bar the door."

Had awa' frae me, D O N A L D.

O WILL you hae ta tartan plaid,
　Or will you hae ta ring, Mattam ?
Or will you hae ta kifs o' me ?
　And dats ta pretty ting, Mattam.
Had awa', bide awa',
　Had awa' frae me, DONALD ;
I'll neither kifs nor hae a ring,
　Nae tartan plaids for me, DONALD.

O fee you not her ponny progues,
    Her fecket plaid, plew, creen, Mattam?
Her twa fhort hofe, and her twa fpoigs,
    And a fhoulter-pelt apeen, Mattam?
Had awa', bide awa',
    Had awa' frae me, DONALD;
Nae fhoulder-belts, nae trinkabouts,
    Nae tartan hofe for me, DONALD.

Hur can pefhaw a petter hongh
    Tan him wha wears ta crown, Mattam;
Herfell hae piftol and claymore
    To flie ta lallant lown, Mattam.
Had awa', had awa',
    Had awa' frae me, DONALD;
For a' your houghs and warlike arms,
    You're no a match for me, DONALD.

Hurfell hae a fhort coat pi pote,
    No trail my feets at rin, Mattam;
A cutty fark of good harn fheet,
    My mitter he be fpin, Mattam.
Had awa', had awa',
    Had awa' frae me, DONALD;
Gae hame and hap your naked houghs,
    And fafh nae mair wi' me, DONALD.

Ye's neir pe pidden work a turn
    At ony kind o' fpin, Mattam,
But fhug your lenno in a fcull,
    And tidel highland fing, Mattam.
Had awa', had awa',
    Had awa', frae me, DONALD;

Your jogging fculls and highland fang
 Will found but harfh wi' me, DONALD.

In ta morning when him rife
 Ye's get frefh whey for tea, Mattam ;
Sweet milk an ream as much you pleafe,
 Far cheaper tan pohea, Mattam.
Had awa', had awa',
 Had awa' frae me, DONALD ;
I winna quit my morning's tea,
 Your whey will ne'er agree, DONALD.

Haper Gallic ye's be learn,
 And tats ta ponny fpeak, Mattam ;
Ye's get a cheefe, an putter-kirn,
 Come wi' me kin ye like, Mattam.
Had awa', had awa',
 Had awa' frae me, DONALD ;
Your Gallic and your Highland chear
 Will ne'er gae down wi' me, DONALD.

Fait ye's pe ket a filder proch
 Pe pigger then the moon, Mattam ;
Ye's ride in curroch ftead o' coach,
 An wow put ye'll pe fine, Mattam.
Had awa', had awa',
 Had awa' frae me, DONALD ;
For a' your Highland rarities
 You're not a match for me, DONALD.

What's tis ta way tat ye'll pe kind
 To a protty man like me, Mattam?
Sae langs claymore pe 'po my fide,
 I'll nefer marry tee, Mattam.

O come awa', run awa',
 O come awa' wi' me, DONALD;
I wadna quit my Highland man;
 Frae Lallands fet me free, DONALD.

The Dreg Song.

I RADE to London yefterday
 On a crucket hay-cock,
Hay-cock, quo' the feale to the eel,.
Cock nae I my tail weel?
Tail-weel, or if hare,
Hunt the dog frae the deer,
Hunt the dog frae the deil-drum;.
Kend ye na JOHNY YOUNG?
JOHN YOUNG and JOHN AULD
Strove about the moniefald;
JEMMY JIMP and JENNY JEUS
Bought a pair of jimp deus,.
Wi' nineteen ftand of feet;
Kend ye nae white breek?
White breek and fteel pike,
Kifs't the lafs behind the dyke,.
Kifs't the lafs behind the dyke,
And fhe whalpet a bairnie;
Hey hou HARRY, HARRY,
Mony a boat fkail'd the ferry,
Mony a boat, mony a fhip;.
Tell me a true note;
True note, true fong,
I've dreg'd o'er long,

O'er lang, o'er late,
Quo' the haddock to the fcate,
Quo' the fcate to the eel,
Cock na I my tail weel?
Tail weel, and gins better,
It's written in a letter:
ANDREW MURRAY faid to MEG,
How many hens hae you wi' egg?
Steek the door and thraw the crock,
Grape you and I'fe look;
Put in your finger in her dock,
And fee gin fhe lays thereout,
She lays thereout days ane,
Sae dis he days twa;
Say dis he days three,
Sae dis he days four,
Quo' the carle o' Aberdour;
Aberdour, Aberdeen,
Grey claith to the green,
Grey claith to the fands,
Trip it, trip it through the lands;
Thro' lands, or if hare,
Hunt the dog frae the deer,
Hunt the deer frae the dog,
Waken, waken, WILLIE TOD,
WILLIE TOD, WILLIE TAY,
Cleckit in the month of May,
Month of May and Averile,
Good fkill o' raifins,
Jentlens and fentlens,
Jeery ory alie;
Weel row'd five men,
As weel your ten,

The oyſters are a gentle kin,
They winna tak unleſs you ſing.
Come buy my oyſters aff the bing,
To ſerve the ſheriff and the king,
And the commons o' the land,
And the commons o' the ſea ;
Hey *benedicete*, and that's good Latin.

I'll chear up my heart.

A S I was a walking ae May-morning,
The fidlers and youngſters were making their game ;
And there I ſaw my faithleſs lover,
And a' my ſorrows returned again.

Well, ſince he is gane, joy gang wi' him ;
It's never be he ſhall gar me complain :
I'll chear up my heart, and I will get another,
I'll never lay a' my love upon ane.

I could na get ſleeping yeſtreen for weeping,
The tears ran down like ſhowers o' rain ;
An' had na I got greiting my heart wad a broken ;
And O ! but love's a tormenting pain.

But ſince he is gane, may joy gae wi' him,
It's never be he that ſhall gar me complain,
I'll chear up my heart, and I will get another ;
I'll never lay a' my love upon ane.

When I gade into my mither's new houſe,
I took my wheel and ſate down to ſpin ;
'Twas there I firſt began my thrift ;
And a' the wooers came linking in.

It was gear he was feeking, but gear he'll na get;
And its never be he that fhall gar me complain,
For I'll chear up my heart, and I'll foon get another;
I'll never lay a' my love upon ane.

R o b i n Red-breaft.

GUDE day now, bonny ROBIN,
  How lang have you been here?
O I have been bird about this bufh,
  This mair then twenty year!

But now I am the fickeft bird,
  That ever fat on brier;
And I wad make my teftament,
  Goodman, if ye wad hear.

Gar tak this bonny neb o' mine,
  That picks upon the corn;
And gie't to the Duke of Hamilton
  To be a hunting-horn.

Gar tak thefe bonny feathers o' mine,
  The feathers o' my neb;
And gie to the Lady o' Hamilton
  To fill a feather-bed.

Gar tak this gude right-leg o' mine,
  And mend the brig o' Tay;
It will be a poft, and pillar gude;
  It will neither bow nor------

And tak this other leg o' mine,
  And mend the brig o' Weir!

It will be a poft and pillar gude;
It'll neither bow nor fteer.

Gar tak thefe bonny feathers o' mine,
The feathers o' my tail;
And gie to the lads o' Hamilton
To be a barn-flail.

And tak thefe bonny feathers o' mine,
The feathers o' my breaft;
And gie to ony bonny lad
That'll bring to me a prieft.

Now in there came my Lady WREN,
With mony a figh and groan;
O what care I for a' the lads,
If my wee lad be gone?

Then ROBIN turn'd him round about,
E'en like a little king;
Go, pack ye out at my chamber-door,
Ye little cutty quean.

Let me in this ae night.

O LASSIE, art thou fleeping yet;
Or are you waking I would wit?
For love has bound me hand and foot,
And I would fain be in, jo.
O let me in this ae night, this ae, ae, ae night,
O let me in this ae night, and I'll ne'er come back again, jo.

The morn it is the term-day,
I maun away, I canna ftay,

O ! pity me before I gae,
And rife and let me in, jo.
O let me, &c.

The night it is baith cauld and weet;
The morn it will be fnaw and fleet,
My fhoon are frozen to my feet,
Wi' ftanding on the plain, jo.
O let me, &c.

I am the laird of windy-wa's,
I come na here without a caufe,
And I hae gotten mony fa's
Upon a naked wame, jo.
O let me, &c.

My father's wa'king on the ftreet,
My mither the chamber-keys does keep;
My chamber-door does chirp and cheep,
And I dare nae let you in, jo.
O gae your ways this ae night, this ae, ae, ae night,
O gae your ways this ae night, for I dare nae let you in, jo.

But I'll come ftealing faftly in,
And cannily make little din;
And then the gate to you I'll find,
If you'll but direct me in, jo.
O let me in, &c.

Caft aff the fhoen frae aff your fee,
Caft back the door up to the weet;
Syne into my bed you may creep,
And do the thing you ken, jo.
O well's me on this ae night, this ae, ae, ae night,
O well's me on this ae night, that ere I let you in, jo.

She let him in fae cannily,
She let him in fae privily,
She let him in fae cannily,
    To do thing you ken, jo.
:O well's me, &c.

But ere a' was done, and a' was faid,
Out fell the bottom of the bed;
The laffie loft her maidenhead,
    And her mither heard the din, jo.
O the devil take this ae night, this ae, ae, ae night,
O the devil take this ae night, that ere I let you in, jo.

Hallow Fair. Tune, Fy let us a' to the Bridal.

THERE's fouth of braw JOCKIES and JENNYS
    Comes weel-bufked into the fair,
With ribbons on their cockernonies,
    And fouth o' fine flour on their hair.
MAGGIE fhe was fae well bufked,
    That WILLIE was ty'd to his bride;
The pounie was ne'er better whifked
    Wi' cudgel that hang frae his fide.
        Sing farrel, &c.

But MAGGIE was wondrous jealous
    To fee WILLIE bufked fae braw;
And SAWNEY he fat in the alehoufe,
    And hard at the liquor did caw.
There was GEORDY that well lov'd his laffie,
    He touk the pint-ftoup in his arms,

VOL. II.   P

And hugg'd it, and faid, Trouth they're faucy
   That loos nae a good father's bairn.
     Sing farrel, &c.

There was WATTIE the muirland laddie,
   That rides on the bonny grey cout,
With fword by his fide like a cadie,
   To drive in the fheep and the knout.
His doublet fae weel it did fit him,
   It fcarcely came down to mid thigh,
With hair pouther'd, hatt and a feather,
   And houfing at courpon and tee.
     Sing farrel, &c.

But bruckie play'd boo to baufie,
   And aff fcour'd the cout like the win':
Poor WATTIE he fell in the caufie,
   And birs'd a the bains in his fkin.
His piftols fell out of the hulfters,
   And were a' bedaubed with dirt;
The folks they came round him in clufters,
   Some leugh, and cry'd, Lad, was you hurt?
     Sing farrel, &c.

But cout wad let nae body fteer him,
   He was ay fae wanton and fkeegh;
The packmans ftands he o'erturn'd them,
   And gard a' the JOCKS ftands a-beech;
Wi' fniring behind and before him,
   For fic is the metal of brutes:
Poor WATTIE, and wae's me for him,
   Was fain to gang hame in his boots.
     Sing farrel, &c.

Now it was late in the ev'ning,
  And boughting-time was drawing near :
The laffes had ftench'd their greening
  With fouth of braw apples and beer:
There was LILLIE, and TIBBIE, and SIBBIE,
  And CEICY on the fpinnell could fpin,
Stood glowring at figns and glafs winnocks,
  But deil a ane bade them come in.
      Sing farrel, &c.

God guide's! faw you ever the like o' it?
  See yonder's a bonny black fwan ;
It glowrs as't wad fain be at us ;
  What's yon that it hads in its hand?
Awa, daft gouk, cries WATTIE,
  They're a' but a rickle of flicks ;
See there is BILL, JOCK, and auld HACKIE,
  And yonder's Mefs JOHN and auld Nick.
      Sing farrel, &e.

Queth MAGGIE, Come buy us our fairing :
  And WATTIE right fleely cou'd tell,
I think thou're the flower of the claughing,
  In trouth now I'fe gie you my fell.
But wha wou'd e'er thought it o' him,
  That e'er he had rippled the lint ?
Sae proud was he o' his MAGGIE,
  Tho' fhe did baith fcalie and fquint.
      Sing farrel, &c.

OUR goodman came hame at e'en,
　　And hame came he:
And then he saw a saddle horse,
　　Where nae horse should be.

O how came this horse here?
　　How can this be?
How came this horse here,
　　Without the leave o' me?

　　A horse! quo' she:
　　Ay, a horse, quo' he.
Ye auld blind dotard carl,
　　Blind mat ye be,
'Tis naething but a bonny milk cow
　　My minny sent to me.

　　A bonny milk cow! quo' he;
　　Ay, a milk cow, quo' she.
Far hae I ridden,
　　And meikle hae I seen,
But a saddle on a cow's back,
　　Saw I never nane,

Our goodman came hame at e'en,
　　And hame came he,
He spy'd a pair of jack boots,
　　Where nae boots should be.

What's this now, goodwife?
　　What's this I see?
How came these boots there
　　Without the leave o' me?

Boots! quo' fhe :
   Ay, boots, quo' he.
Shame fa' your cuckold face,
   And ill mat ye fee,
It's but a pair of water ftoups
   The cooper fent to me.

   Water ftoups ! quo' he ;
   Ay, water ftoups, quo fhe.
Far hae I riden,
   And farer hae I gane,
But filler fpurs on water ftoups,
   Saw I never nane.

Our goodman came hame at e'en,
   And hame came he,
And then he faw a fword,
   Where a fword fhould nae be :

What's this now, goodwife?
   What's this I fee ?
O how came this fword here,
   Without the leave o' me?

   A fword ! quo' fhe,
   Ay, a fword, quo' he.
Shame fa' your cuckold face,
   And ill mat you fee,
It's but a parridge fpurtle
   My minnie fent to me.

Weil, far hae I ridden,
   And muckle hae I feen ;
But filler handed fpurtles
   Saw I never nane.

Our goodman came hame at e'en,
   And hame came he ;
There he fpy'd a powder'd wig,
   Where nae wig fhould be :

What's this now, goodwife ?
   What's this I fee ?
How came this wig here,
   Without the leave o' me ?

    A wig ! quo' fhe ;
    Ay, a wig, quo' he.
Shame fa' your cuckold face,
   And ill mat you fee,
'Tis naething but a clocken-hen
   My minnie fent to me.

    Clocken hen ! quo' he :
    Ay, clocken-hen, quo' fhe,
Far hae I ridden,
   And muckle hae I feen,
But powder on a clocken hen
   Saw I never nane.

Our goodman came hame at e'en,
   And hame came he,
And there he faw a muckle coat,
   Where nae coat fhou'd be ?

O how came this coat here ?
   How can this be ?
How came this coat here
   Without the leave o' me ?

    A coat ! quo' fhe :
    Ay, a coat, quo' he.

Ye auld blind dotard carl,
  Blind mat ye. be,.
It's but a pair of blankets
  My minnie fent to me.

  Blankets ! quo' he :
    Ay, blankets, quo' fhe.
Far hae I ridden,
  And muckle have I feen;
But buttons upon blankets
  Saw I never nane..

Ben went our goodman,
  And ben went he,
And there he fpy'd a fturdy man,
  Where nae man fhou'd be :

How came this man here?
  How can this be ?·
How came this man here,
  Without the leave o' me?:

  A man ! quo' fhe :
    Ay, a man, quo' he.
Poor blind body,
  And blinder mat ye be,.
It's a new milking maid,.
  My mither fent to me..

  A maid ! quo' he :
    Ay, a maid, quo' fhe.
Far hae I ridden,
  And muckle hae I feen,
But lang-bearded maidens
  I faw never nane.

The Nurse's Song.

HOW dan dilly dow,
   How den dan,
Weel were your minny
   An ye were a man.

Ye wad hunt and hawk,
   And had her o' game,
And water your dady's horse,
   I' the mill dam.

How dan dilly dow,
   How dan flours,
Ye's ly i' your bed
   Till eleven hours.

If at ele'en hours you lift to rise,
Ye's hae your dinner dight in a new guise;
   La'rick's legs and titlens toes
   And a' sic dainties my Mannie shall hae.

                              Da Capo.

Kind-hearted NANCY.

I'LL go to the green wood,
   Quo' NANCY, quo' NANCY,
I'll go to the green wood,
   Quo' kind hearted NANCY.

O what an I come after you?
   Quo' WILSY, quo' WILSY,

O what an I come after you?
  Quo' fla cow'rdly WILSY.

And what gif ye come back again?
  Quo' NANCY, quo' NANCY;
And what gif ye come back again?
  Quo' kind hearted NANCY.

But what gif I fhou'd lay thee down?
  Quo' WILSY, quo' WILSY;
What gif I should lay thee down?
  Quo' fla cow'rdly WILSY.

And what gif I can rife again?
  Quo' NANCY, quo' NANCY;
And what gif I can rife again?
  Quo' kind hearted NANCY.

O but what if I get you wi' bairn?
  Quo' WILSY, quo' WILSY;
O what gif I get you wi' bairn?
  Quo' fla cow'rdly WILSY.

If you can get it I can bear't,
  Quo' NANCY, quo' NANCY;
If you can get it I can bear't,
  Quo' kind hearted NANCY.

Whar'l we get a cradle till't?
  Quo' WILSY, quo' WILSY;
Whar'l we get a cradle till't?
  Quo' fla cow'rdly WILSY.

There's plenty o' wood in Norway,
  Quo' NANCY, quo' NANCY;

There's plenty o' wood in Norway,
  Quo' kind hearted NANCY.

Whar'l we get a cradle-belt?
  Quo' WILSY, quo' WILSY;
Whar'l we get a cradle-belt?
  Quo' fla cow'rdly WILSY.

Your garters and mine,
  Quo' NANCY, quo' NANCY;
Your garters and mine,
  Quo' kind hearted NANCY.

Then whar'l I tye my beaftie to?
  Quo' WILSY, quo' WILSY;
Then whar'l I tye my beaftie to?
  Quo' fla cow'rdly WILSY.

Tye him to my muckle tae,
  Quo' NANCY, quo' NANCY;
Tye him to my muckle tae,
  Quo' kind hearted NANCY.

O what gif he fhould run awa'?
  Quo' WILSY, quo' WILSY;
O what gif he fhould run awa'?
  Quo' fla cow'rdly WILSY.

Deil gae wi' you, fteed and a',
  Quo' NANCY, quo' NANCY:
Deil gae wi' you, fteed and a',
  Quo' kind hearted NANCY.

Bide ye yet.

GIN I had a wee houfe and a canty wee fire,
A bony wee wife to praife and admire;
A bonny wee yardie afide a wee burn,
Farewell to the bodies that yamer and mourn.

And byde ye yet, and byde ye yet,
Ye little ken what may betide you yet;
Some bonny wee bodie may be my lot,
And I'll ay be canty wi' thinking o't.

When I gang afield, and come hame at e'en,
I'll get my wee wifie fou neat and fou clean;
And a bonnie wee bairnie upon her knee,
That will cry papa or daddy to me.

And bide ye yet, &c.

And if there fhould happen ever to be,
A difference a'tween my wee wifie and me;
In hearty good humour although fhe be teaz'd,
I'll kifs her and clap her until fhe be pleas'd.

And bide ye yet, &c.

Ranting Roving Lad.

MY love was born in Aberdeen,
The bonnieft lad that e'er was feen;
O he is forced frae me to gae,
Over the hills and far away.

O he's a ranting roving laddie;
O he's a brifk and a benny laddie;

Betide what will, I'll get me ready,
And follow the lad wi' the Highland plaidie.

I'll fell my rock, my reel, my tow,
My gude grey mare and hacket cow,
To buy my love a tartan plaid,
Becaufe he is a roving blade.

O he's a ranting roving laddie,
O he's a brifk and a bonny laddie,
Betide what will I'll get me ready,
To follow the lad wi' the Highland plaidy.

Let him gang.

IT was on a Sunday,
  My love and I did meet,
Which caufed me on Monday
To figh and to weep ;
O to weep is a folly,
Is a folly to me,
Sen he'll be mine nae langer,
Let him gang---farewell he.

Let him gang, let him gang,
Let him fink, let him fwim ;
If he'll be my love nae langer,
Let him gang---farewell him ;
Let him drink to Rofemary,
And I to the thyme ;
Let him drink to his love,
And I unto mine.

For my mind fhall never alter,
    And vary to and fro ;
I will bear a true affection
    To the young lad I know ;
Let him gang, let him gang,
    Let him fink or let him fwim ;
If he'll be my love nae langer,
    Let him gang---farewell him.

Tune. JENNY *dang the weaver.*

A S I came in by Fifherraw,
    Muffelburgh was near me;
I threw aff my mufsle pock,
    And courted wi' my deary.

O had her apron bidden down,
    The kirk wad ne'er ha kend it ;
But fince the word's gane thro' the town,
    My dear I canna mend it.

But ye maun mount the cutty-ftool,
    And I maun mount the pillar;
And that's the way that poor folks do,
    Becaufe they hae nae filler.

Up ftairs, down ftairs,
    Timber ftairs fears me.
I thought it lang to' ly my lane,
    When I'm fae near my dearie.

THE shepherd's wife cries o'er the lee,
    Come hame will ye, come hame will ye:
The shepherd's wife cries o'er the lee,
    Come hame will ye again een, jo?

What will ye gie me to my supper,
    Gin I come hame, gin I come hame?
What will ye gie me to my supper,
    Gin I come hame again een, jo?

Ye's get a panfu' of plumpin parrage;
    And butter in them, and butter in them;
Ye's get a panfu' of plumpin parrage,
    Gin ye'll come hame again een, jo.

Ha, ha, how, it's naething that dow;
    I winna come hame, and I canna come hame.
Ha, ha, how, it's naething that dow;
    I winna come hame again een, jo.

    [*The two first verses are to be sung here and after.*]

Ye's get a cock well totled i' the pat,
    An ye'll come hame, an ye'll come hame;
Ye's get a cock well totled i' the pat,
    An ye'll come hame again een, jo.

    [*The third verse for the chorus, ha, ha,* &c.]

Ye's get a hen well boil'd i' the pan;
    An ye'll come hame, an ye'll come hame,
Ye's get a hen well boil'd i' the pan,
    An ye'll come hame again een, jo.

A well made bed, and a pair of clean sheets,
    An ye'll come hame, an ye'll come hame ;
A well made bed, and a pair of clean sheets,
    An ye'll come hame again een, jo.
      Ha, ha, &c.

A pair of white legs, and a good cogg-wame,
    An ye'll come hame, an ye'll come hame ;
A pair of white legs, and a good cogg-wame,
    An ye'll come hame again een, jo.

Ha, ha, how, that's something that dow ;
    I will come hame, I will come hame.
Ha, ha, how, that's something that dow ;
    I'll haste me hame again een, jo.

[*The two first verses of this song, are to be sung before the* 4, 5 6, 7, *and* 8*th verses, as before the* 3d, *and the* 4*th after them by way of chorus.*]

Old King C o u l.

OLD King Coul was a jolly old soul,
    And a jolly old soul was he :
Old King Coul he had a brown bowl,
And they brought him in fidlers three :
And every fidler was a very good fidler,
And a very good fidler was he.
Fidell-didell, fidell-didell, with the fidlers three ;
And there's no a lass in a' Scotland
Compared to our sweet MARJORIE.

Old King Cou l was a jolly old foul,
And a jolly old foul was he:
Old King Coul he had a brown bowl,
And they brought him in pipers three:
Ha-didell, how-didell, ha-didell, how-didell, with the
　　　pipers three :
Fidell didell, fidell, didell, with the fidlers :
And there's no a lafs in a' Scotland
Compared to our fweet MARJORIE.

Old King Coul was a jolly old foul,
And a jolly old foul was he ;
Old King Coul he had a brown-bowl,
And they brought him in harpers three:
Twingle-twangle, twingle-twangle, went the harpers;
Ha-didell, how-didell, ha-didell, how-didell, went the
　　　pipers;
Fidell-didell, fidell-didell, went the fidlers ;
And there's no a lafs in a' Scotland
Compared to our fweet MARJORIE.

Old King Coul was a jolly old foul,
And a jolly old foul was he :
Old King Coul he had a brown-bowl,
And they brought him in trumpeters three.
Twarra-rang, twarra-rang, went the trumpeters;
Twingle-twangle, twingle-twangle, went the harpers;
Ha-didell, how-didell, went the pipers ;
Fidell-didell, fidell-didell, went the fidlers three :
And there's no a lafs in a' Scotland
Compared to our fweet MARJORIE.

Old King Cou l was a jolly old foul,
And a jolly old foul was he :

Old King Co u l he had a brown-bowl,
And they brought him in drummers three.
Rub-a-dub rub-a-dub, with the drummers;
Twarra-rang, twarra-rang, with the trumpeters;
'Twingle-twangle, twingle-twangle, with the harpers;
Ha-didell, how-didell, with the pipers;
Fidell-didell, fidell-didell, with the fidlers three:
And there's no a lafs in a' Scotland
Compared to our fweet MARJORIE.

The Miller of Dee.

THERE was a jolly miller once
    Liv'd on the water of Dee;
He wrought and fang frae morn to night;
    No lark more blyth than he:
And this the burden of his fang
    For ever us'd to be,
I care for no body, no not I,
    Since no body cares for me.

I live by my mill, God blefs her,
    She's kindred, child and wife;
I would not change my ftation,
    For any other in life.
No lawyer, furgeon or doctor,
    E'er had a groat from me;
I care for no body, no not I,
    If no body cares for me.

When fpring begins his merry career,
    Oh how his heart grows gay;

Q 3

No fummer's drought alarms his fears,
 Nor winter's fad decay :
No forefight mars the miller's joy,
 Who's wont to fing and fay,
Let others toil from year to year,
 I live from day to day.

Thus like the miller bold and free
 Let us rejoice and fing,
The days of youth are made for glee,
 And time is on the wing.
This fong fhall pafs from me to thee,
 Along this jovial ring ;
Let heart and voice and all agree
 To fay, Long live the king.

The Turnimfpike.

HER fel pe Highland fhentleman,
 Pe auld as Pothwel prig, man ;
And mony alterations feen
 Amang the Lawland whig, man.
  Fal lal, &c.

Firft when her to the Lowlands came,
 Nain fell was driving cows, man :
There was nae laws about hims narfe,
 About the preeks or troufe, man.
  Fal lal, &c.

Nain fell did wear the philapeg,
 The plaid prik't on her fhouder ;

The gude claymore hung pe her pelt,
　The piftol fharg'd wi' pouder.
　　Fal lal, &c.

But for whereas thefe curfed preels,
　Wherewith mans narfe be lockit,
O hon, that ere fhe faw the day !
　For a' her houghs pe prokit.
　　Fal lal, &c.

Every thing in the Highlands now
　Pe turn't to alteration ;
The fodger dwal at our door cheek,
　And that's te great vexation.
　　Fal lal, &c.

Scotland be turn't a Ningland now,
　And laws pring on the cadger :
Nain fell wad durk him for hur deeds,
　But oh fhe fears de' fodger.
　　Fal lal, &c.

Another law came after that,
　Me never faw the like, man ;
They mak a lang road on the crund,
　And ca' him turnimfpike, man.
　　Fal, lal &c.

And wow fhe pe a ponny road,
　Like Louden corn rigs, man ;
Where twa carts may gang on her,
　And no break others legs, man.
　　Fal lal, &c.

They fharge a penny for ilka hors,
　In troth they'l be nae fheaper,

For nought but gaen upo' the crund,
  And they gie me a paper.
    Fal lal, &c.

They tak the hors than pe the head,
  And there they mak them ftand, man,
I tell'd them that I feen the day
  They had na fic command, man.
    Fal lal, &c.

Nae doubts nain-fell maun draw his purs,
  And pay them what him's like, man:
I'll fee a fhudgement on his ftore,
  That filthy turnimfpike, man.
    Fal lal, &c.

But I'll awa to the Highland hills,
  Whare nere a ane fall turn her;
And no come near your turnimfpike,
  Unlefs it pe to purn her.
    Fal lal, &c.

P a t i e's Wedding.

As PATIE came up frae the glen,
  Drivin his wedders before him,
He met bonny MEG ganging hame,
  Her beauty was like for to finore him.
O dinna ye ken, bonny MEG,
  That you and I's gaen to be married?
I rather had broken my leg,
  Before fic a bargain mifcarried.

Na, PATIE—O wha's tell'd you that ?
    I think that of news they've been fcanty,
That I fhould be married fo foon,
    Or yet fhould hae been fae flantly :
I winna be married the year,
    Suppofe I were courted by twenty ;
Sae, PATIE, ye need nae mair fpear,
    For weel a wat I dinna want ye.

Now, MEGGIE, what maks ye fae fweer ?
    Is't caufe that I henna a maillin ?
The lad that has plenty o' gear
    Need ne'er want a half or a hail ane:
My dad has a good gray mare,
    And yours has twa cows and a filly ;
And that will be plenty o' gear,
    Sae MAGGIE, be no fae ill-willy.

Indeed, PATIE, I dinna ken,
    But firft ye maun fpeir at my daddy :
You're as well born as BEN,
    And I canna fay but I'm ready.
There's plenty o' yarn in clues,
    To make me a coat and a jimpy,
And plaiden enough to be trews,
    Gif ye get it, I fhanna fcrimp ye.

Now fair fa' ye, my bonny MEG,
    I's let a wee fnacky fa' on you.
May my neck be as lang as my leg,
    If I be an ill hufband unto you.
Sae gang your way hame e'now,
    Make ready gin this day fifteen days,

And tell your father the news,
 That I'll be his son in great kindness.

It was nae lang after that,
 Wha came to our bigging but PATIE,
Weel dreſt in a braw new coat,
 And wow but he thought himſelf pretty.
His bannet was little frae new,
 In it was a loop and a ſlitty,
To tie in a ribbon ſae blue,
 To bab at the neck o' his coaty.

Then PATIE came in wi' a ſtend,
 Said, Peace be here to the bigging.
You're welcome, quo' WILLIAM, come ben,
 Or I wiſh it may rive frae the rigging.
Now draw in your ſeat and ſit down,
 And tell's a' your news in a hurry;
And haſte ye, MEG, and be done,
 And hing on the pan wi' the berry.

Quoth PATIE, My news is nae thrang;
 Yeſtreen I was wi' his Honour;
I've taen three riggs of bra' land,
 And hae bound myſel under a bonour:
And now my errand to you
 Is for MEGGY to help me to labour;
I think you maun gie's the beſt cow,
 Becauſe that our haddin's but ſober.

Well, now for to help you through,
 I'll be at the coſt of the bridal;
I'ſe cut the craig of the ewe
 That had amaiſt deid of the ſide-ill,

And that 'ill be plenty of bree,
  Sae lang as our well is nae reifted,
To all the good neighbours and we,
  And I think we'll ne be that ill feafted.

Quoth PATIE, O that'il do well,
  And I'll gie you your brofe in the morning,
O' kail that was made yeftreen,
  For I like them beft in the forenoon,
Sae TAM the piper did play,
  And ilka ane danc'd that was willing,
And a' the lave they ranked through,
  And they held the ftoupy ay filling.

The auld wives fat and they chew'd,
  And when that the carles grew nappy,
They danc'd as weel as they dow'd,
  Wi' a crack o' their thumbs and a kappie.
The lad that wore the white band,
  I think they cau'd him JAMIE MATHER,
And he took the bride by the hand,
  And cry'd to play up MAGGIE LAUDER.

Tune, *Fy gar rub her o'er wi' ftrae.*

DEAR ROGER, if your JENNY geck,
  And anfwer kindnefs with a flight,
Seem unconcern'd at her neglect,
  For women in a man delight :
But them defpife who're foon defeat,
  And with a fimple face give way
To a repulfe ;—then be not blate,
  Pufh bauldly en, and win the day,

When maidens, innocently young,
  Say aften what they never mean,
Ne'er mind their pretty lying tongue,
  But tent the language of their een:
If thefe agree, and fhe perfift
  To anfwer all your love with hate,
Seek elfewhere to be better bleft,
  And let her figh when 'tis too late.

Tune, *Polwart on the Green.*

THE dorty will repent,
  If lovers heart grow cauld,
And nane her finiles will tent,
  Soon as her face looks auld.

The dawted bairn thus takes the pet,
  Nor eats, though hunger crave,
Whimpers and tarrows at its meat,
  And's laugh'd at by the lave.

They jeft it till the dinner's paft;
  Thus by itfelf abus'd,
The fool-thing is oblig'd to faft,
  Or eat what they've refus'd.

Tune, *O dear mother, what fhall I do?*

O DEAR PEGGY, love's beguiling,
  We ought not to truft to finiling;
Better far to do as I do,
Left a harder luck betide you.

'Laffes, when their fancy's carry'd,
Think of nought but to be marry'd:
Running to a life deftroys
Heartfome, free, and youthfu' joys.

Tune, *How can I be fad on my wedding day?*

HOW fhall I be fad, when a hufband I hae,
That has better fenfe than ony of thae
Sour weak filly fellows, that ftudy, like fools,
To fink their ain joy and make their wives fnools?
The man who is prudent ne'er lightlies his wife,
Or with dull reproaches encourages ftrife ;
He praifes her virtue, and ne'er will abufe
Her for a fmall failing, but find an excufe.

Tune, *Cauld kale in Aberdeen.*

CAULD be the rebels caft,
Oppreffors bafe and bloody,
I hope we'll fee them at the laft
Strung a' up in a woody.
Blefs'd be he of worth and fenfe,
And ever high his ftation,
That bravely ftands in the defence
Of confcience, king and nation.

Tune, *Mucking of Geordy's byre.*

THE laird wha in riches and honour
 Wad thrive, fhould be kindly and free,
Nor rack the poor tenants, who labour
 To rife àboon poverty :
Elfe like the pack-horfe that's unfother'd,
 And burden'd, will tumble down faint;
Thus virtue by hardfhip is fmother'd,
 And rackers aft tine their rent.

PEGGY, now the king's come,
 PEGGY, now the King's come,
Thou may dance, and I fhall fing,
 PEGGY, fince the King's come.
Nae mair the hawkies fhall thou milk,
But change thy plaiding coat to filk,
And be a lady of that ilk,
 Now, PEGGY, fince the King's come.

Tune, *Happy Clown.*

HID from himfelf, now by the dawn,
 He ftarts as frefh as rofes blawn,
And ranges o'er the heights and lawn
 After his bleeting flocks,

Healthful, and innocently gay,
He chants and whiftles out the day,
Untaught to fmile, and then betray,
    Like courtly weathercocks.

Life happy, from ambition free,
Envy, and vile hypocrifie,
Where truth and love with joy agree,
    Unfully'd with a crime ;
Unmov'd with what difturbs the great,
In propping of their pride and ftate,
He lives, and unafraid of fate,
    Contented fpends his time.

For the Love of JEAN.

JOCKY faid to JENNY, JENNY wilt thou do't,
  Ne'er a fit, quoth JENNY, for my tocher good,
For my tocher good I winna marry thee :
E'en's ye like, quoth JOCKY, ye may let it be.

  I ha'e gowd and gear, I ha'e land enough,
I ha'e feven good owfen ganging in a pleugh,
Ganging in a pleugh, and linkan o'er the lee,
And gin ye winna tak me, I can let ye be.

  I ha'e a good ha' houfe, a barn and a byar,
A peat-ftack 'fore the door, will make a rantin fire ;
I'll make a rantin fire, and merry fall we be,
And gin ye winna tak me, I can let ye be.

JENNY faid to JOCKY, Gin ye winna tell,
Ye fall be the lad, I'll be the lafs myfell :
Ye're a bonny lad, and I'm a laffie free ;
Ye're welcomer to tak me than to let me be.

Tune, *The Bridegroom greets.*

WHEN the fheep are in the fauld, and the ky at hame,
And a' the warld to fleep are gane ;
The waes of my heart fa's in fhowers frae my eye,
When my gudeman lyes found by me.

Young JEMMY loo'd me well, and he fought me for
    his bride,
But faving a crown he had naething befide ;
To make that crown a pound, my JEMMY gade to fea,
And the crown and the pound were baith for me.

He had nae been awa' a week but only twa,
When my mother fhe fell fick, and the cow was ftoun
    awa' ;
My father brake his arm, and my JEMMY at the fea,
And auld ROBIN GREY came a courting me.

My father coudna work, and my mother coudna fpin,
I toil'd day and night, but their bread I coudna win ;
Auld ROB maintain'd them baith, and wi' tears in his ee,
Said, JENNY for their fakes, O marry me.

My heart it faid nay, I look'd for JEMMY back ;
But the wind it blew high, and the fhip it was a wreck,
The fhip it was a wreck, why didna JEMMY die ?
And why do I live to fay waes me ?

Auld R o b i n argued fair, tho' my mother didna fpeak,
She looked in my face till my heart was like to break ;
So they gi'ed him my hand, tho' my heart was in the fea,
And auld R o b i n G r e y is gudeman to me.

I hadna been a wife a week but only four,
When fitting fae mournfully at the door,
I faw my J e m m y's wreath, for I coudna think it he,
'Till he faid, I'm come back for to marry thee.

O fair did we greet, and muckle did we fay ;
We took but ae kifs, and we tore ourfelves away ;
I wifh I were dead ! but I'm no like to die,
And why do I.live to fay waes me ?

I gang like a ghaift; and I carena to fpin ;
I darena think on.J e m m y, for that wou'd be a fin ;
But I'll do my beft a gude wife to be,
For auld R o b i n G r e y is kind unto me.

W a t t y and M a d g e.

In imitation of W i l l i a m and M a r g a r e t.

'T W A S at the fhining mid-day hour,
    When all began to gaunt,
That hunger rugg'd at W a t t y's breaft,
    And the poor lad grew faint.

His face was like a bacon ham
    That lang in reek had hung,

And horn-hàrd was his tawny hand
   That held his hazel rung.

So wad the fäfteft face appear
   Of the maift drefſy ſpark,
And ſuch the hands that lords wad hae,
   Were they kept cloſe at wark.

His head was like a heathery buſh
   Beneath his bonnet blew,
On his braid cheeks, frae lug to lug,
   His bairdy briflles grew.

But hunger, like a gnawing worm,
   Gade rumbling through his kyte,
And nothing now but folid gear
   Cou'd give his heart delyte.

He to the kitchen ran with ſpeed,
   To his lov'd MADGE he ran,
Sunk down into the chimney-nook
   With viſage four and wan.

Get up, he cries, my criſhy love,
   Support my finking faul
With fomething that is fit to chew,
   Be't either het or caul.

This is the how and hungry hour,
   When the beft cures for grief
Are cog-fous of the lythy kail,
   And a good junt of beef.

Oh WATTY, WATTY, MADGE replies,
   I but o'er juftly trow'd

Your love was thowlefs, and that ye
    For cake and pudding woo'd.

Bethink thee, WATTY, on that night,
    When all were faft afleep,
How ye kifs'd me frae cheek to cheek,
    Now leave thefe cheeks to dreep.

How cou'd ye ca' my hurdies fat,
    And comfort of your fight?
How cou'd you roofe my dimpled hand,
    Now all my dimples flight?

Why did you promife me a fnood,
    To bind my locks fae brown?
Why did you me fine garters heght,
    Yet let my hofe fa' down?

O faithlefs WATTY, think how aft
    I ment your farks and hofe!
For you how many bannocks flown,
    How many cogues of brofe!

But hark!—the kail-bell rings, and I
    Maun gae link aff the pot;
Come fee, ye hafh, how fair I fweat;
    To ftegh your guts, ye fot.

The grace was faid, the mafter ferv'd;
    Fat MADGE return'd again,
Blyth WATTY raife and rax'd himfell,
    And fidg'd he was fae fain.

He hy'd him to the favoury bench,
    Where a warm haggies ftood,

And gart his gooly through the bag
    Let out its fat heart's blood.

And thrice he cry'd, Come eat, dear MADGE,
    Of this delicious fare;
Syne claw'd it off moſt cleverly,
    Till he could eat nae mair.

FRAGMENTS

OF

COMIC

AND

HUMOUROUS SONGS.

Mucking of GEORDIE's byre.

THE mucking of GEORDY's byre,
  And fhooling the grupe fae clean,
  Has gard me weit my cheiks
And greit with baith my een.
  It was ne'er my father's will,
  Nor yet my mother's defire,
  That e'er I fhould file my fingers,
  Wi' mucking of GEORDY's byre.

The moufe is a merry beaft,
  And the moudewort wants the een:
But the warld fhall ne'er get wit
  Sae merry as we ha'e been.
  It was ne'er, &c.

Bonny Dundee.

O HAVE I burnt, or have I flain?
   Or have I done aught injury?
I've gotten a bonny young laffie wi' bairn,
   The bailie's daughter of bonny Dundee.
Bonny Dundee, and bonny Dundafs,
   Where fhall I fee fae bonny a lafs?
Open your ports, and let me gang free,
   I maun ftay nae langer in bonny Dundee.

Galla-Water.

BRAW, braw lads of Galla water,
   O braw lads of Galla-water,
I'll kilt my coats below my knee,
   And follow my love through the water.
Sae fair her hair, fae brent her brow,
   Sae bonny blue her een, my dearie,
Sae white her teeth, fae fweet her mou',
   I aften kifs her till I'm wearie.

O'er yon bank, and o'er yon brae,
   O'er yon mofs amang the hether,
I'll kilt my coats aboon my knee,
   And follow my love through the water.
Down amang the broom, the broom,
   Down amang the broom, my dearie;
The laffie loft her filken fnood,
   That gard her greet till fhe was wearie.

Gae to the ky wi' me, JOHNY.

GAE to the ky wi' me, JOHNY,
  Gae to the ky wi' me;
Gae to the ky wi' me, JOHNY,
  And I'll be merry wi' thee.
And was she not wordy of kisses,
  And was she not wordy of three,
And was she not wordy of kisses,
  That gaed to the ky wi' me?
  Gae to the ky, &c.

I have a house to big,
  And another that's like to fa',
I have a lassie wi' bairn,
  Which grieves me warst of a'.
  Gae to the ky, &c.

If that she be now wi' bairn,
  As I trow weel she be,
I have an auld wife to my mither,
  Will doudle it on her knee.
  Gae to the ky, &c.

Brose and Butter.

GI'E my love brose, brose,
  Gi'e my love brose and butter,
Gi'e my love brose, brose,
  Yestreen he wanted his supper.

JENNY fits up in the laft,
    JOCKY wad fain hae been at her,
There came a wind out of the waft,
    Made a' the windows to clatter.
      Gi'e my love, &c.

A goofe is nae good meat,
    A hen is bofs within,
In a pye there's muckle deceit,
    A pudding it is a good thing.
      Gi'e my love, &c.

JENNY's Bawbie.

AND a' that e'er my JENNY had,
    My JENNY had, my JENNY had;
A' that e'er my JENNY had,
    Was ae bawbie.
There's your plack, and my plack,
And your plack, and my plack,
And my plack and your plack,
And JENNY's bawbie.
    And a' that e'er, &c.

We'll put it a' in the pint-ftoup,
The pint-ftoup, the pint-ftoup,
We'll put it in the pint-ftoup,
And birle't a' three.
    And a' that e'er, &c.

Cauld kale in Aberdeen.

CAULD kale in Aberdeen,
  And caſtocks in Strabogie ;
But yet I fear they'll cook o'er ſoon,
  And never warm the cogie.
The laſſes about Bogie gicht,
Their limbs they are ſae clean and tight,
That if they were but girded right,
  They'll dance the reel of Bogie.

Wow, ABERDEEN, what did you mean,
  Sae young a maid to woo, Sir ?
I'm ſure it was nae mows to her,
  Whate'er it was to you, Sir ;
For laſſes now are no ſae blate,
But they ken auld folks out o' date,
And better playfare can they get,
  Than caſtocks in Strabogie.

Cock up your Beaver.

WHEN firſt my dear JOHNY came to this town,
  He had a blue bonnet, it wanted the crown ;
But now he has gotten a hat and a feather,
Hey, my JOHNY lad, cock up your beaver.
Cock up your beaver, cock up your beaver,
Hey, my JOHNY lad, cock up your beaver ;
Cock up your beaver, and cock it nae wrang,
We'll a' to England ere it be lang.

John, come kiſs me now.

JOHN, *come kiſs me now, now, now,*
O JOHN *come kiſs me now,*
JOHN *come kiſs me by and by,*
And make nae mair ado.
Some will court and compliment,
And make a great ado,
Some will make of their goodman,
And ſae will I of you.
JOHN, *come kiſs,* &c.

When ſhe came ben ſhe bobbit.

WHEN ſhe came ben ſhe bobbit,
And when ſhe came ben ſhe ſobbit.
And when ſhe came ben ſhe kiſt COCKPEN,
And then deny'd that ſhe did it.

And was nae COCKPEN right ſawcy,
And was nae COCKPEN right ſawcy?
He len'd his lady to gentlemen,
And he kiſt the collier laſſie.

And was nae COCKPEN right able,
And was nae COCKPEN right able?
He left his lady with gentlemen,
And he kiſt the laſs in the ſtable.

O are you wi' bairn, my chicken?
O are you wi' bairn, my chicken?
O if I am not, I hope to be,
E'er the green leaves be fhaken.

I wifh that you were dead, Goodman.

I WISH that you were dead, goodman,
*   And a green fod on your head, goodman,*
*   That I might ware my widowhead,*
*   Upon a ranting highlandman.*

There's fax eggs in the pan, goodman,
There's fax eggs in the pan, goodman,
There's ane to you, and twa to me,
And three to our JOHN HIGHLANDMAN.
    I wifh, &c.

There's beef into the pat, goodman,
There's beef into the pat, goodman,
The banes for you, and the brew for me,
And the beef for our JOHN HIGHLANDMAN.
    I wifh, &c.

There's fax horfe in the ftable, goodman,
There's fax horfe in the ftable, goodman,
There's ane to you, and twa to me,
And three to our JOHN HIGHLANDMAN.
    I wifh, &c.

There's fax ky in the byre, goodman,
There's fax ky in the byre, goodman,

There's nane o' them yours, but there's twa of them
   mine,
And the lave is our JOHN HIGHLANDMAN's.
   I wiſh, &c.

Whiſtle o'er the lave o't.

MY mither ſent me to the well,
   She had better gane herſell,
I got the thing I dare nae tell,
   Whiſtle o'er the lave o't.

My mither ſent me to the ſea,
For to gather muſles three;
A ſailor lad fell in wi' me,
   Whiſtle o'er the lave o't.

The Grey Cock.

O SAW ye my father, or ſaw ye my mother,
   Or ſaw ye my true love JOHN?
I ſaw not your father, I ſaw not your mother,
   But I ſaw your true love JOHN.

It's now ten at night, and the ſtars gie nae light:
   And the bells they ring ding, dong,
He's met wi' ſome delay, that cauſeth him to ſtay;
   But he will be here ere lang.

The furly auld carl did naething but fnarl,
　　And Johny's face it grew red;
Yet tho' he often figh'd, he ne'er a word reply'd,
　　Till all were afleep in bed.

Up Johny rofe, and to the door he goes,
　　And gently tirled the pin;
The laffie taking tent, unto the door fhe went,
　　And fhe open'd and let him in.

And are ye come at laft, and do I hold ye faft?
　　And is my Johny true?
I have nae time to tell, but fae lang's I like my fell,
　　Sae lang fall I love you.

Flee, flee up, my bonny grey cock,
　　And craw whan it is day;
Your neck fhall be like the bonny beaten gold,
　　And your wings of the filver grey.

The cock prov'd falfe, and untrue he was,
　　For he crew an hour o'er foon;
The laffie thought it day when fhe fent her love away,
　　And it was but a blink of the moon.

The WREN; or, LENNOX's Love to BLAN-TYRE.

THE WREN fche lyes in care's bed,
　　In care's bed, in care's bed;
The WREN fcho lyes in care's bed,
　　In meikle dule and pyne---O.

S 3

Quhen in came ROBIN Red-breaſt,
  Red-breaſt, Red-breaſt ;
Quhen in came ROBIN Red-breaſt,
  Wi' ſuccar-ſaps and wyne---O.

Now, maiden, will ye taſte o' this,
  Taſte o' this, taſte o' this ;
Now, maiden, will you taſte o' this?
  It's ſuccar-ſaps and wyne---O.
Na, ne'er a drap, ROBIN,
  ROBIN, ROBIN ;
Na, ne'er a drap, ROBIN,
  Gin it was ne'er ſo fine---O.

* * * * * *

And quhere's the ring that I gied ze,
  That I gied ze, that I gied ze ;
And quhere's the ring that I gied ze,
  Ze little cutty quean---O
I gied it till a ſoger,
  A ſoger, a ſoger,
I gied it till a ſoger,
  A kynd ſweet-heart o' myne---O.

WILL ze go to the wood? quo' FOZIE MOZIE ;
  Will ze go to the wood? quo' JOHNIE REDNOZIE ;
Will ze go to the wood? quo' FOSLIN 'ene ;
Will ze go to the wood? quo' brither and kin.

What to do there? quo' FOZIE MOZIE ;
What to do there? quo' JOHNIE REDNOZIE ;
What to do there? quo' FOSLIN 'ene ;
What to do there? quo' brither and kin.

SCOTS SONGS. 211

To flay the WREN, quo FOZIE MOZIE:
To flay the WREN, quo' JOHNIE REDNOZIE:
To flay the WREN, quo' FOSLIN 'ene:
To flay the WREN, quo' brither and kin.

What way will ze get her hame? quo' FOZIE MOZIE;
What way will ze get her hame? quo' JOHNIE RED-
    NOZIE;
What way will ze get her hame? quo' FOSLIN 'ene;
What way will ze get her hame? quo' brither and kin.

We'll hyre carts and horfe, quo' FOZIE MOZIE:
We'll hyre carts and horfe, quo' JOHNIE REDNOZIE:
We'll hyre carts and horfe, quo' FOSLIN 'ene:
We'll hyre carts and horfe, quo' brither and kin.

What way will we get her in? quo' FOZIE MOZIE;
What way will we get her in? quo' JOHNIE RED-
    NOZIE;
What way will we get her in? quo' FOSLIN 'ene;
What way will ze get her in? quo' brither and kin.

We'll drive down the door-cheeks, quo' FOZIE MOZIE:
We'll drive down the door-cheeks, quo' JOHNIE RED-
    NOZIE:
We'll drive down the door-cheeks, quo' FOSLIN 'ene:
We'll drive down the door-cheeks, quo' brither and kin:

I'll hae a wing, quo' FOZIE MOZIE:
I'll hae anither, quo' JOHNIE REDNOZIE:
I'll hae a leg, quo' FOSLIN 'ene:
And I'll hae anither, quo' brither and kin.

Luftie MAYE.

O LUSTIE MAYE, with FLORA Quëen,
    The balmy drops from PHOEBUS fheen,
Prelufant beams before the day,
Before the day, the day ;
By thee, DIANA, groweth green,
    Through gladnefs of this luftie MAYE,
    Through gladnefs of this luftie MAYE *.

Then AURORA that is fo bright,
To weful hearts he cafts great light,
    Right pleafantly before the day, &c.
And fhows and fhades forth of that light,
    Through gladnefs of this luftie MAYE,
    Through gladnefs of this luftie MAYE.

Birds, on their boughs, of every fort,
Send forth their notes, and make great mirth,
    On banks that bloom on every bray, &c.
And fares and flyes o'er field and firth,
    Through gladnefs of this luftie MAYE,
    Through gladnefs of this luftie MAYE.

All lovers hearts that are in care,
To their ladies they do repair,
    In frefh mornings before the day, &c.
And are in mirth ay more and more,
    Through gladnefs of this luftie MAYE,
    Through gladnefs of this luftie MAYE.

* The firft verfe of this fong is cited in a book intitled; The
Complaint of Scotland, &c. printed at St Andrews in 1548;
whereby it appears to have been a current old Scots fong in
the reign of JAMES V.

Of every monith in the year,
To mirthful MAYE there is no peer,
  Her glift'ring garments are fo gay, &c.
Your lovers all make merry cheer,
  Through gladnefs of this luftie MAYE,
  Through gladnefs of this luftie MAYE.

Tune, JOHN ANDERSON *my Jo.*

WHEN I was a wee thing,
  And juft like an elf,
All the meat that e'er I gat,
  I laid upon the fhelf.

The rottens and the mice
  They fell into a ftrife,
They wadnae let my meat alane
  Till I gat a wife.

And when I gat a wife,
  She wadnae bide therein,
Till I gat a hurl-barrow
  To hurle her out and in.

The hurl-barrow brake,
  My wife fhe gat a fa';
And the foul fa' the hurl-barrow,
  Cripple wife and a'.

She wadnae eat nae bacon,
  She wadnae eat nae beef,
She wadnae eat nae lang-kail,
  For fyling o' her teeth:

But she wad eat the bonnie bird,
　　That sits upon the tree :.
Gang down the burn, Davie, love,
　　And I sall follow thee.

Wali fu fa the Cat.

As I came down bonny Tweed-side,
　　I heard and I wist nae what ;
I heard ae wife say to anither,
　　O waly fu fa' the cat !

O waly fu fa the cat !
　　For she has bred muckle wanease ;
She has op'ned the amry door,
　　And has eaten up a' our bit cheese.

She has eaten up a' the bit cheese ;
　　O' the bannocks she's no left a mote ;
She has dung the hen aff her eggs ;
　　And she's drown'd in the sowin-boat.

O waly fu fa the cat !
　　I kend she wad never do grace ;
She has pist i' the backet of sa't ;
　　And has dung the bit fish aff the brace.

She has dung the bit fish aff the brace ;
　　And it's fallen i' the maister-can ;
And now it has sic a stink,
　　It'll pizen the silly good man.

Dainty DAVIE *.

O LEEZE me on your curly pow,
  Dainty DAVIE, dainty DAVIE;
Leeze me on your curly pow,
  Mine ain dainty DAVIE.

It was in and through the window broads,
  And a' the tirlie wirlies o'd;
The sweetest kifs that e'er I got,
  Was frae my dainty DAVIE.
O leeze me on your curly pow, &c.

It was down amang my dady's peafe,
  And underneath the cherry-trees;
O there he kift me as he pleas'd,
  For he was mine ain dear DAVIE.
O leeze me on your curly pow, &c.

When he was chas'd by a dragoon,
  Into my bed he was laid down;
I thought him wordy o' his room,
  And he's ay my dainty DAVIE.
O leeze me on your curly pow, &c.

* * * * * * *

HEY how JOHNY lad, ye're no fae kind's ye fud hae
    been,
Hey how JOHNY lad, ye're no fae kind's ye fud hae been;

* The following fong was made upon Mefs David William-
fon, on his getting with child the Lady Cherrytree's daughter, while the foldiers were fearching the houfe to apprehend
him for a rebel.

Sae weel's ye might hae touzled me, and sweetly pried my
    mow bedeen;
Hey how Johny lad, ye're no sae kind's ye sud hae been;

My father he was at the pleugh, my mither she was at
    the mill,
My billie he was at the mofs, and no ane near our
    sport to spill;
The feint a body was therein, ye need na fley'd for
    being seen;
Hey how Johny lad, ye're no sae kind's ye sud hae been.

But I maun hae anither joe, whase love gangs never out
    o' mind,
And winna let the mament pafs, when to a lafs he can
    be kind;
Then gang yere wa's to Blinking Bess, nae mair for
    Johny sal she green;
Hey how Johny lad, ye're no sae kind's ye sud hae
    been.

JOHNY JOHNSTON.

O Johny Johnston was my love,
    But wha wad e'er hae thought it o' him?
He's left me for a tocher'd lafs,
    A dirty slut unwordy o' him.

But to the bridal I sall gang,
    Although I'm sure I was nae bidden:
I care nae tho' they a' should cry,
    Hech, fee, sirs, yonder comes the dirdam.

When I came to the bridal-houfe,
  Wow, but the flut had little 'havens !
For ay fhe rave, and rugged at,
  And licked a' the creechy gravins.

A gentleman that fate neeft me,
  Was fpearing wha was't that was aught her;
Indeed, fir, I think fhame to tell,
  She's fic a filly body's daughter.

The bride fhe minted wi' a bane,
  And grin'd at me becaufe I faid it ;
She faid, fays fhe, fay that again,
  And I'fe gar you make ae thing twa o't.

I trow then when the bride faw this,
  She bade my love come for to pleafe me;
He came, and bade me chufe my fpring,
  And faid, fays he, what's this that grieves you?

I'm neither griev'd nor fad, fays I,
  And that I'll let you ken to eafe you,
I'll dance, fae will I, gif I like ;
  And ye's tire firft, Sir, I'fe affure you.

But when the bedding came at e'en,
  Wow, but the houfe was in a fteery;
The bride was frighted fair for fear,
  That I wad take awa' her deary.

My bonny love gae flow to bed,
  He kifs'd her——but 'twas for the fafhion;
And fyne he glowr'd at my white fkin,
  And fyne he figh'd, and rued the bargain.

HOW lang have I a batchelor been,
  This twa and twenty year?
How aft have I a-wooing gane?
  Tho' I came never the near.

For, NANNIE she says, she winna hae me,
  I look sae like a cloun;
But by my footh, I'm as good as herfel,
  Sae I's ne'er fash my thumb.

She says, if I could loup and dance,
  As TAM the miller can;
Or cut a caper like the taylor,
  She wad like me than.

By my word it's daffin to lie,
  My joints were ne'er fo nimble;
The taylor he has naething to mind,
  But his bodkin, shears, and thimble.

And how do you do, my little wee NAN,
  My lamb and slibrikin moufe?
And how does your father and mother do,
  And a' the good folks i' the houfe?

I think nae shame to shaw my shapes;
  I'se warrand ye'll guefs my errand;
You maun gang wi' me, my fair maid,
  To marry you, fir, I warrand.

But, maun belongs to the king himfell,
  But no to a country cloun;
Ye might have said, wi' your leave, fair maid,
  And letten your maun alane.

O fee but how fhe mocks me now,
 She fcoffs me and does fcorn;
The man that marries you, fair maid,
 Maun rife right foon i' the morn.

But fare ye weil, and e'en's you like,
 For I can get anither.
He lap on his horfe at the back o' the dyke,
 And gaed hame to tell his mither.

When NAN faw that, fhe wad na wait,
 But fhe has ta'en the taylor;
For when a lafs gets the lad fhe likes
 'Tis better far than filler.

But when he heard that NANSE was tint,
 As he fat on yon know ;
He ruggit his hair, he blubber'd and grat,
 And to a ftane daddit his pow.

His mither came out, and wi' the difhclout,
 She daddit about his mow;
The deil's i' the chield, I think he's gane daft,
 Get up, ye blubbering fow.

If ever there was an ill wife i' the warld,
 It was my hap to get her;
And by my hap, and by my luck,
 I had been better butt her.

I wifh I had been laid i' my grave,
 When I got her to marriage !
For, the very firft night the ftrife began,
 And fhe gae me my carriage.

I fcoured awa to Edinborow-town,
 And my cutty-brown together;
And there I bought her a braw new-gown,
 I'm fure it coft fome filler.

Ilka ell o't was a crown,
 'Twas better than her marriage :
But becaufe it was black, and it was na brown,
 For that I got my carriage.

When I faw naething her wad mend,
 I took her to the foreft ;
The very firft wood that I came to,
 Green-holan was the neareft ;

There I paid her baith back and fide,
 Till a' her banes play'd clatter ;
And a' the bairns gathered round about,
 Cry'd, fy goodman have at her.

A S I gaed to the well at e'en,
 As any honeft auld woman will do,
 The carl then he follow'd me,
As auld carles will do.
  He woo'd me, and loo'd me,
  A wally how he woo'd me !
  But yet I winna tell to you,
  How the carl woo'd me.

 As I fat at my wheel at e'en,
As any honeft auld woman fhou'd do,
 The carl he came in to me,
As auld carles will do.
  He woo'd me, and loo'd me, &c.

As I gaed to my bed at e'en,
As any other honeſt auld woman wou'd do,
   The carl then he came to me,
As auld carles will do.
    He woo'd me, and loo'd me, &c.

Lumps of Pudding.

MY daddy he ſteal'd the miniſter's cow,
   And 'a' we weans gat puddings anew ;
The dirt crap out, as the meat gaed in,
And wow ſic puddings as we gat then !
   Sic lumps o' puddings, ſic dads o' bread,
   They ſtack in my throat, and maiſt were my dead.

As I gaed by the miniſter's yard,
I ſpied the miniſter kiſſing his maid :
Gin ye winnae believe, cum here and ſee
Sic a braw new coat the miniſter gied me.
   Sic lumps o' puddings, &c.

Birks of Abergeldie.

BONNIE laſſie, will ye go,
   Will ye go, will ye go,
Bonnie laſſie, will ye go
   To the birks o' Abergeldie ?
Ye ſhall get a gown of ſilk,
   A gown of ſilk, a gown of ſilk,
Ye ſhall get a gown of ſilk,
   And coat of calimancoe.

Na, kind Sir, I dare nae gang,
  I dare nae gang, I dare nae gang,
Na, kind Sir, I dare nae gang;
  My minnie fhe'll be angry.
Sair, fair wad fhe flyte,
  Wad fhe flyte, wad fhe flyte,
Sair, fair wad fhe flyte,
  And fair wad fhe ban me.

KEEP the country, bonny laffie,
  Keep the country, keep the country,
Keep the country, bonny laffie;
  Lads will a' gie gowd for ye:
Gowd for ye, bonny laffie,
  Gowd for ye, gow'd for ye,
Keep the country, bonny laffie,
  Lads will a' gie gowd for ye.

AND fare ye weel, my auld wife,
  Sing bum, be bery, bum:
Fare ye weel, my auld wife,
  Sing bum, bum, bum,
Fare ye weel, my auld wife,
The fteerer up o' ftrunt and ftrife;
  The malt's aboon the meal the night,
  Wi' fome, fome, fome.

And fare ye weel, my pyke-ftaff,
  Sing bum, be bery bum;
Fare ye weel, my pyke-ftaff,
  Sing, bum, bum, bum:

Fare ye weel, my pyke-ftaff,
Wi' you nae mair my wife I'll baff;
    The malt's aboon the meal the night
    Wi' fome, fome, fome.

WILL ye go to Flanders, my MALLY—O?
    Will ye go to Flanders, my bonnie MALLY—O?
There we'll get wine and brandy,
    And fack and fugar-candy;
Will ye go to Flanders, my MALLY—O?

Will ye go to Flanders, my MALLY—O?
And fee the chief commanders, my MALLY—O?
    You'll fee the bullets fly, and the foldiers how they die,
And the ladies loudly cry, my MALLY—O!

TIBBY FOWLER o' the glen,
    There's o'er mony wooing at her;
She has lovers nine or ten,
    There's o'er mony wooing at her:

Wooing at her, kiffing at her,
    Clapping at her, cannae get her;
Shame fa' her filthy fnout,
    There's o'er mony wooing at her.

Kirk wad let me be.

I AM a poor filly auld man;
  And hirpling o'er a tree ;
Zet fain, fain kifs wad I,
  Gin the kirk wad let me be;

Gin a' my duds were aff,
  And a' hail claes on,
O I could kifs a zoung lafs,
  As weel as ony man.

Blink over the Burn, fweet BETTY.

IN fimmer I mawed my meadows,
  In harveft I fhure my corn,
In winter I married a widow,
  I wifh I was free the morn.

Blink over the burn, fweet BETTY,
  Blink over the burn to me :
O it is a thoufand pities
  · But I was a widow for thee.

Green grows the Rafhes.

GREEN grows the rafhes—O,
  Green grows the rafhes—O :
The feather-bed is no fae faft
As a bed amang the rafhes.

We're a' dry wi' drinking o't,
  We're a' dry wi' drinking o't ;
The parſon kiſt the fidler's wife,
  And he cou'd na preach for thinking o't.
    Green grows, &c.

The down-bed, the feather-bed,
  The bed amang the raſhes—O ;
Yet a' the beds is na ſae ſaft
  As the bellies o' the laſſes.—O.

O Tʜɪs is my departing time !
  For here nae langer maun I ſtay :
There's not a friend or foe of mine
  But wiſhes that I were away.

What I hae done for lack o' wit,
  I never, never can recal !
I hope you're a' my friends as yet :
  Good-night and joy be wi' you all.

I Hae layen three herring a' fa't :
  Bonnie laſs, gin ze'll take me, tell me now :
And I hae brow'n three pickles o' ma't :
  And I cannae cum ilka day to woo ;
    To woo, to woo, to lilt and to woo :
    And I cannae cum ilka day to woo.

I ha'e a wee ca'f that wad fain be a cow :
　Bonnie laſſie, gin ze'll take me, tell me now :
I hae a wee gryce that wad fain be a fow :
　And I cannae cum ilka day to woo ;
　　To woo, to woo, to lilt and to woo ;
　　And I cannae cum ilka day to woo.

　　　*　*　*　*　*　*

Up in the Morning early.

THERE gaed a fair maiden out to walk,
　In a morning of July :
She was fair, bonnie, ſweet, and young ;
　But met wi' a lad unruly.

He took her by the lilly-white hand ;
　He ſwore he loo'd her truly :
The man forgot, but the maid thought on,
　O it was in the month of July !

Kiſt the Streen.

On the 'late Duke of Argyle.

O AS I was kiſt yeſtreen !
　O as I was kiſt yeſtreen !
I'll never forget till the day that I die,
Sae mony braw kiſſes his Grace gae me.

My father was ſleeping, my mither was out,
And I was my lane, and in came the Duke :

I'll never forget till the day that I die,
Sae mony braw kisses his Grace gae me.

Kist the streen, kist the streen,
Up the Gallowgate, down the Green:
I'll never forget till the day that I die,
Sae mony braw kisses his Grace gae me.

* * * * * *

Tune, *Fy, gar rub her o'er wi' strae.*

LOOK up to Pentland's tow'ring tops,
    Buried beneath great wreaths of snaw,
O'er ilka cleugh, ilk scar and slap,
    As high as ony Roman wa'.

Driving their baws frae whins or tee,
    There's no nae gowfer to be seen,
Nor douffer fowk wysing a-jee
    The byast bouls on Tamson's green.

Then fling on coals, and ripe the ribs,
    And beek the house baith but and ben,
That mutchken stoup it hads but dribs,
    Then let's get in the tappit hen.

Good claret best keeps out the cauld,
    And drives away the winter soon;
It makes a man baith gash and bauld,
    And lifts his saul beyond the moon.

Leave to the gods your ilka care,
    If that they think us worth their while,
They can a rowth of blessings spare,
    Which will our fashious fears beguile.

For what they have a mind to do,
   That will they do, fhould we gang wood;
If they command the ftorms to blaw,
   Then upo' fight the hailftains thud.

But foon as ere they cry, be quiet,
   The blatt'ring winds dare nae mair move,
But cour into their caves, and wait
   The high command of fupreme JOVE.

Let neift day come as it thinks fit,
   The prefent minute's only ours;
On pleafure let's employ our wit,
   And laugh at fortune's fecklefs powers †.

WHEN I gaed to the mill my lane,
   For to ground my malt,
The miller-laddie kift me;
   I thought it was nae fau't.
What though the laddie kift me,
   When I was at the mill!
A kifs is but a touch;
   And a touch can do na ill.

O I loo the miller-laddie!
   And my laddie lues me;
He has fic a blyth look,
   And a bonnie blinking ee.

---

† For the remainder of this fong, fee page 42d of the prefent volume.

What though the laddie kiſt me,
　　When I was at the mill !
A kiſs is but a touch ;
　　And a touch can do na ill.

DONALD COWPER and his man
　　They've gane to the fair ;
They've gane to court a bonny laſs,
　　But fint a ma was there :
But he has gotten an auld wife,
　　And ſhe's come hirpling hame ;
And ſhe's fa'n o'er the buffet-ſtool,
　　And brake her rumple-bane.
　　Sing, Hey DONALD, *how* DONALD,
　　　　Hey DONALD COWPER ;
　　He's gane awaʳ to court a wife,
　　　　And he's come hame without her.

Tune, *Green Sleeves.*

AS I walk'd by myſelf, I ſaid to myſelf,
　　And myſelf ſaid again to me,
Look well to thyſelf, take care of thyſelf,
　　For no body cares' for thee.

Then I anſwer'd to myſelf, and ſaid to myſelf,
　　With the ſelf-ſame repartee,
Look well to thyſelf, or not to thyſelf,
　　It's the ſelf-ſame thing to me.

VOL. II.　　　　　　　　U

MY wife's a wanton wee thing,
   My wife's a wanton wee thing,
My wife's a wanton wee thing ;
   She'll never be guided by me.

She play'd the loon e'er fhe was married,
She play'd the loon e'er fhe was married,
She play'd the loon e'er fhe was married ;
   She'll do't again e'er fhe die.

LOGAN-WATER and Logan-braes—
   I helped a bonnie laffie on wi' her claiths;
Firft wi' her ftockings, and then wi' her fhoon ;
And fhe gave me the glaiks when a' was done.

But had I kend what I ken now,
I fhould have bang'd her belly fou,
Her belly fou, and her apron up ;
And hae fhew'd her the way to Logan-kirk.

SYMON BRODIE had a cow :
   The cow was loft, and he cou'd na find her ;
When he had done what man cou'd do,
   The cow came hame, and the tail behind her.
     Honeft, auld SYMON BRODIE,
     Stupid, auld, doited bodie ;
     I'll awa' to the North Countrie,
     And fee my ain dear SYMON BRODIE.

SYMON BRODIE had a wife,
 And wow but she was braw and bonnie ;
She took the dish-clout aff the bink,
 And prin'd it to her cockernonie.
  Honeft, auld SYMON BRODIE, &c.

*   *   *   *   *   *

Barm.

I'LL trip upon trenchers, I'll dance upon dishes ;
 My mither fent me for barm, for barm :
And through the kirk-yard I met wi' the laird,
 The filly, poor body could do me no harm.

But down i' the park, I met with the clerk,
 And he gaed me my barm, my barm.

*   *   *   *   *   *

The bonnie lafs of Anglefey.

OUR king he has a fecret to tell,
 And ay we'll keep it muft and be ;
The English lords are coming down,
 To dance and win the victory.

Our king has cry'd a noble cry,
 And ay we'll keep it muft and be ;
Gar faddle ye, and bring to me,
 The bonnie lafs of Anglefey.

Up fhe ftarts as white as the milk,
　　Between him and his company;
What is the thing I hae to afk,
　　If I fhould win the victory?

Fifteen ploughs but and a mill,
　　I'll gie thee till the day thou die;
And the faireft knight in a' my court,
　　To chufe thy hufband for to be.

She's ta'en the fifteen lords by the hand,
　　Saying, Will ye come dance with me?
But on the morn, at ten o'clock,
　　They gave it o'er moft fhamefully.

Up then rofe the fifteenth lord;
　　I wat an angry man was he;
Laid by frae him his belt and fword,
　　And to the floor gaed manfully.

He faid, My feet fhall be my dead,
　　Before fhe win the victory;
But before 'twas ten o'clock at night,
　　He gaed it o'er as fhamefully.

The Dainty Downby.

THERE's a farmer near hard by,
　　Sent out his daughter to keep the ky,
Sent out his daughter to keep the ky,
　　In the green of the Dainty Downby.

This laſſie being of a noble mind,
She went to the garden to pu' a pickle thyme,
She went to the garden to pu' a pickle thyme,
  In the garden of the Dainty Downby.

Little did ſhe ken that the laird was at hame,
Little did ſhe ken that the laird was at hame,
Little did ſhe ken that the laird was at hame,
  The laird of the Dainty Downby.

He has ta'en her by the milk-white hand,
He has ta'en her by the grafs-green fleeve,
He has made her to be at his command,
  In the green of the Dainty Downby.

O go hame ! go hame, and tell your father this,
Go hame, go hame, and tell your father this,
Go hame, go hame, and tell your father this,
  What ye've gotten in the Dainty Downby.

Her father is to this young laird gone,
For to pay fome rents that he was owing,
For to pay fome rents that he was owing,
  To the Laird of the Dainty Downby.

O how is your daughter MARG'RET ! he faid,
O how is your daughter MARG'RET ! he faid,
O how is your daughter MARG'RET, he faid,
  Since ſhe was in the Dainty Downby ?

Gae gar her come and fpeak to me,
Gae gar her come and fpeak to me,
Gae gar her come right fpeedily,
  To me in the Dainty Downby.

When this laſſie before this young laird came,
Her lover baith grew pale and wan :
O MARG'RET, MARG'RET ! you've lain with a man,
  Since you was in the Dainty Downby.

O kind Sir ! you may well underſtand,
Since you made me to be at your command,
You made me to be at your command ;
  And wo to your Dainty Downby !

O MARG'RET, MAR'GRET ! gif I be the man,
If I be the man that has done ye the wrang,
I ſhall be the man that will raiſe you again,
  Since you was in the Dainty Downby.

Then he has call'd upon his vaſſals all,
He has call'd on them baith great and ſmall ;
Then he has made her there, before them all,
  The Lady of the Dainty Downby.

The TOD.

THERE dwells a TOD on yonder craig,
    And he's a TOD of might—a ;
He lives as well on his purchaſe,
    As ony laird or knight—a.

JOHN ARMSTRANG ſaid unto the TOD,
    An ye come near my ſheep—a,
The firſt time that I meet wi' you,
    It's I will gar ye greet—a.

The TOD ſaid to JOHN ARMSTRANG again,
    Ye dare na be ſae bauld—a ;
For'n I hear ony mair o' your din,
    I'll worry a' the ſheep o' your fauld—a.

The Tod he hies him to his craig,
   And there fits he fu' croufs—a ;
And for Johnie Armstrang, and a' his tykes,
   He does not care a loufe—a.

Reckle Mahudie.

MITHER.

WHERE will we get a wife to you?
   My auld fon Reckle Mahudie.

SON.

Wha but Maggie a-yont the burn,
   She'll make a wife right gudie.

MITHER.

I fear fhe'll be but a fober wife,
   My auld fon Reckle Mahudie.

SON.

I believe you'd hae me feek a king's dochter,
   But foul fa' me if I dudie.

MITHER.

O what'll you hae to your wadden feaft?
   My auld fon Reckle Mahudie.

SON.

A pint of brofe and a good fa't herring,
   It'll make a feaft right gudie.

MITHER.

I fear it'll be but a fober feaft,
  My auld fon RECKLE MAHUDIE.

SON.

I believe you'd hae me hae baith fodden and roaft,
  But foul fa' me if I dudie.

MITHER.

O wha'll you hae at your wadden,
  My auld fon RECKLE MAHUDIE?

SON.

Wha but MAGGIE an myfell,
  It'll make a wadden right gudie.

MITHER.

I fear it'll be but a fober wadden,
  My auld fon RECKLE MAHUDIE.

SON.

I believe you'd hae me hae an hoft of folk,
  But foul fa' me gin I dudie.

THE prettieft laird in a' the weft,
  And that was BONNYMOON;
And TEUKSTON was courageous,
Cry'd for a wanton quean:

And BOYSAC he was tender,
And might nae byde nae wear;

And yet he came courageously,
Without or dread or fear.
   O Boysac gin ye die,
   O Boysac gin ye die,
   O I'fe put on your winding fheet,
   Fine Hollan it fhall be.

I'd rather hae Red-Caftle
And a red rofe in his hand,
Before I'd hae ye, Boysac,
Wi' thretty ploughs of land.
   O Boysac, gin ye die,
   O Boysac, gin ye die,
   O I'fe put on your winding fheet,
   Fine Hollan it fhall be.

———————————————

* * * * * * *

AND there fhe's lean'd her back to a thorn,
   Oh, and alas-a-day! Oh, and alas-a-day!
And there fhe has her baby born,
   Ten thoufand times good night, and be wi' thee.

She has houked a grave ayont the fun,
   Oh, and alas-a-day! Oh, and alas-a-day!
And there fhe has buried the fweet babe in,
   Ten thoufand times good night, and be wi' thee.

And fhe's gane back to her father's ha',
   Oh, and alas-a-day! Oh, and alas-a-day!
She's counted the leeleft maid o' them a',
   Ten thoufand times good night and be wi' thee.

* * * * * * * * * *

O look not fae fweet, my bonny babe,
  Oh, and alas-a-day! Oh, and alas-a-day!
Gin ze fmyle fae ze'll finyle me dead;
  Ten thoufand times good night and be wi' thee.

* * * * * * * * * *

Tune, *Pecfe Strae.*

THE country fwain that haunts the plain,
  Driving the lightfome plow;
At night though tired, with love all fired,
  He views the laffie's brow.
Whan morning comes, inftead of drums,
  The flails flap merrilie;
To raife the maids out o' their beds,
  To fhake the peafe-ftrae.

Fair JENNY raife, pat on her claife,
  Syne tuned her voice to fing;
She fang fae fweet, wi' notes compleat,
  Gard a' the echoes ring;
And a' the males lay by their flails,
  And dance moft merrily;
And blefs the hour that fhe had power
  To fhake the peafe-ftrae.

The mufing fwain difturb'd in brain,
  Faft to her arms he flew,
And ftrave a while, then wi' a finile,
  Sweet JENNY red in hue,

She faid right aft, I think ye're daft,
    That tempts a laffie fae;
Ye'll do me wrang, pray let me gang,
    And fhake the peafe-ftrae.

My heart, faid he, fair wounded be,
    For thee, my JENNY fair;
Without a jeft, I get nae reft,
    My bed it proves a fnare.
Thy image fine, prefents me fyne,
    And takes a' reft me frae;
And while I dream, in your efteem
    You reckon me your fae.

Which is a fign ye will be mine,
    Dear JENNY fay nae na;
But foon comply, or elfe I die,
    Sae tell me but a flaw,
If you can love, for none above
    Thee I can fancy fae,
I would be bleft if I but wift,
    That you would fhake my ftrae.

Then JENNY fmil'd, faid, You're beguil'd,
    I canna fancy thee;
My minny bauld, fhe would me fcauld,
    Sae dinna die for me.
But yet I own I am near grown,
    A woman; fince its fae,
I'll marry thee, fyne you'll get me
    To fhake your peafe-ftrae.

GLOSSARY.

A

GLOSSARY,

OR

EXPLANATION of the *Scotch* Words.

Some general rules, shewing wherein many Southern *and* Northern *words are originally the same, having only a letter changed for another, or sometimes one taken away or added.*

I. In many words ending with an l after an a or u, the l is rarely founded.

Scots.	English.
A'Ba,	ALL, Ball.
Ca,	Call.
Fa,	Fall.
Ga,	Gall.
Ha,	Hall.
Sma,	Small.
Sta,	Stall.
Wa,	Wall.
Fou, or Fu,	Full.
Pou, or Pu,	Pull
Woo, or U,	Wool.

II. The l changes to a, w, or u, after o, or a, and is frequently funk before another confonant; as,

Scots.	English.
BAwm, Bauk,	BAlm. Baulk.
Bouk,	Bulk.
Bow,	Boll.
Bowt,	Bolt.
Caff,	Calf.

Scots.	English.
Cow,	Coll, or Clip.
Faut,	Fault.
Faufe,	Falfe.
Fowk,	Folk.
Fawn,	Fallen.
Gowd,	Gold.
Haff,	Half.
How,	Hole, or Hollow.
Howms,	Holms.
Maut,	Malt.
Pow,	Poll.
Row,	Roll.
Scawd,	Scold
Stown,	Stoln.
Wawk,	Walk.

III. An o before ld, changes to a or au; as,

Scots.	English.
AUld, Bauld	OLD. Bold.
Cauld,	Cold.
Fauld,	Fold.
Hald, or had,	Hold.
Sald,	Sold.
Tald,	Told.
Wad,	Would.

IV. The o, oe, ow, is changed
to a, ae, or ai; as,

Scots.	English.
A E, or ane,	O NE.
Aeten,	Oaten.
Aff,	Off.
Aften,	Often.
Aik,	Oak.
Aith,	Oath.
Ain, or awn,	Own.
Alane,	Alone.
Amaift,	Almoft.
Amang,	Among.
Airs,	Oars.
Aites,	Oats.
Apen,	Open.
Awner,	Owner.
Bain,	Bone.
Bair,	Bore.
Baith,	Both.
Blaw,	Blow.
Braid,	Broad.
Claith,	Cloth.
Craw,	Crow.
Drap,	Drop.
Fae,	Foe.
Frae,	Fro, or from.
Gae,	Go.
Gaits,	Goats.
Grane,	Groan.
Haly,	Holy.
Hale,	Whole.
Halefome,	Wholefome.
Hame,	Home.
Hait, or het,	Hot.
Laith,	Loath.
Laid,	Load.
Lain, or len,	Loan.
Lang,	Long.
Law,	Low.
Mae,	Moe.
Maift,	Moft.
Mair,	More.
Mane,	Moan.
Maw,	Mow.
Na,	No.
Nane,	None.

Scots.	English.
Naithing,	Nothing.
Pape,	Pope.
Rae,	Roe.
Rair,	Roar.
Raip,	Rope.
Raw,	Row.
Saft,	Soft.
Saip,	Soap.
Sair,	Sore.
Sang,	Song.
Slaw,	Slow.
Snaw,	Snow.
Strake,	Stroak.
Staw,	Stole.
Stane,	Stone.
Saul,	Soul.
Tae,	Toe.
Taiken,	Token.
Tangs,	Tongs.
Tap,	Top.
Thrang,	Throng.
Wae,	Woe.
Wame,	Womb.
Wan,	Won.
War,	Worfe.
Wark,	Work.
Warld,	World.
Wha,	Who.

V. The o or u is frequently
changed into i; as,

Scots.	English.
A Nither,	A Nother.
Bill,	Bull.
Birn,	Burn.
Brither,	Brother.
Fit,	Foot.
Fither,	Fother.
Hinny,	Honey.
Ither,	Other.
Mither,	Mother.
Nits,	Nuts.
Nile,	Nofe.
Pit,	Put.
Rin,	Run.
Sin,	Sun.

A

ABLINS, perhaps.
Aboon, above.
Abbey, the precincts of the Abbey of Holyroodhouse at Edinburgh, is a sanctuary for debitors, who are sometimes humourously termed, Abbey-Lairds.
Abee, let abee, let alone, defift, ceafe.
Aefauld, fincere, without guile.
Afore, before.
Afterhind, thereafter.
Ahint, behind.
Air, long fince, early. Air up, foon up in the morning.
Airts, points of the compafs.
A'ms, alms.
Amry, a cup-board.
Anew, enough.
Ark, a corn or meal cheft.
Arles, earneft of a bargain.
Afe, afhes.
Afteer, ftirring.
At ains, or anes, at once, at the fame time.
Attour, befides.
Awfome, frightful, terrible.
A-will, of itfelf, of its own accord.
Auld-farran, ingenious,

Auftie, auftere, harfh.
Aurglebargin, to contend and wrangle.
A-wie, a little.
Ayont, beyond.

B.

BADRANS, a cat.
Baid, ftaid, abode.
Bagrie, trafh.
Bairns, children.
Band, bond.
Bang, is fometimes an action of hafte. We fay, he or it came wi' a bang. —A bang alfo means a great number. *Of cuftomers fhe had a bang.*
Bangl'd up, fwelled.
Bangfter, a bluftering roaring perfon.
Bannocks, a fort of bread thicker than cakes, and round.
Baps, rolls of bread.
Barken'd, when mire, blood, &c. hardens upon a thing like bark.
Barlikhood, a fit of drunken angry paffion.
Barrow-trams, the ftaves of a hand-barrow.
Batts, cholic.
Bawbee, halfpenny.
Barley-brie, ale or beer.
Bauch, forry, indifferent.

Bawfy, baw fand-fac'd, is a cow or horfe with a white face.

Bawty, a dog's name.

Bedeen, immediately, in hafte.

Begoud, began.

Begrutten, all in tears.

Beik, to bafk.

Beild, or beil, a fhelter.

Bein, or been, wealthy. A been houfe, a warm well furnifhed one.

Beit, or beet, to help, repair.

Begunk, a trick.

Bells, bubbles.

Belt, a girdle.

Beltan, the 3d of May, or Rood-day.

Ban, curfe.

Ben, the inner room of a houfe.

Bennifon, blefling.

Benfell, or benfail, force.

Bend, draught.

Bent, the open field.

Beuk, baked.

Beurith, fomewhat in the mean time.

Bickering, fighting, running quickly; fchool-boys battling with ftones.

Bigg, build. Bigget, built. Biggings, buildings.

Biggonet, a linen cap or coif.

Billy, brother.

Borroftown, a town or borrough.

Byre, a byar, a cow-ftall.

Birks, birch-trees.

Birle, to drink. Common people joining their farthings for purchafing liquor, they call it, birling a bawbee.

Birn, a burnt mark.

Birns, the ftalks of burnt heath.

Birr, force, flying fwiftly with a noife.

Birs'd, bruifed.

Bittle, or beetle, a wooden mell for beating hemp, or a fuller's club.

Black-a-vic'd, of a black complexion.

Blae, pale blue, the colour of the fkin when bruifed.

Blazind leather, tanned leather.

Blaftum, beguile.

Blate, bafhful.

Blatter, a rattling noife.

Bleech, to blanch or whiten.

Bleer, to make the eye water.

Bleez, blaze.

Blether, foolifh difcourfe. Bletherer, a babler. Stammering is called blethering.

Blin, ceafe. Never blin, never have done.

Blinkan, the flame rifing and falling, as of a lamp when the oil is exhaufted. Twinkling.

Blink, a glance of the eye, a ray of light.

Boak, or boke, vomit.

Boal, a little prefs or cupboard in the wall.

Bodin, or bodden, provided or furnished.

Bodle, one fixth of a penny Englifh.

Blind-harrie, a game at romps.

Bodword, an ominous meffage. Bodwords are now ufed to exprefs ill-natured meffages.

Blob, a drop.

Boglebo, hobgoblin or fpectre.

Bonny, beautiful.

Bonywalys, toys, gewgaws.

Bofs, empty.

Bouk, bulk, carcafe.

Bow, or boll, a meafure equal to a fack.

Brankand, gay.

Bouze, to drink.

Brochen, a kind of watergruel of oat-meal, butter, and honey.

Brae, the fide of a hill, bank of a river.

Braird, the firft fprouting of corns.

Brander, a gridiron.

Brands, calves of the legs.

Brankan, prancing, a capering.

Branks, wherewith the ruftics bridle their horfes.

Brattle, noife, as of horfefeet.

Brats, rags.

Braw, brave, fine in apparel.

Breeks, breeches.

Brecken, fearn.

Brent-brow, fmooth high forehead.

Bridal, wedding.

Brigs, bridges.

Brifs, to prefs.

Brock, a badger.

Broo, broth.

Brie, foup, fauce.

Browden, fond,

Browfter, brewer.

Browft, a brewing.

Bruliment, a broil.

Buckled, yoked in marriage.

Bucky, the large fea-fnail. A term of reproach, when we exprefs a crofs-natured fellow, by a thrawn bucky.

Buff, nonfenfe. As, He blether'd buff.

Bught, the little fold where the ews are inclofed at milking-time.

Buller, to bubble. The motion of water at a fpring head, or noife of a rifing tide.

Bumbazed, confufed. Made to ftare and look like an idiot.

Bung, completely fuddled, as it were to the bung.

Bunkers, a bench, or fort

of long low chefts that
ferve for feats.

Bumbler, a bungler.

Burn, a brook.

Bufk, to deck, drefs.

Buftine, fuftin (cloth)·

But, often for without; as,
But feed or favour.

Bykes or bikes, nefts or hives
of bees.

Bygane, bypaft.

By-word, a proverb.

Bees, humours, fancies.

Bun, the pofteriors.

But and ben, this and the
other end of the houfe.

Blyth, chearful.

Broach, a brooch or clafp.

Balow, hufh : *Bas, la le
loup*; peace, there is the
·wolf. A phrafe to ftill
children.

Bobit, curtfied.

Belyve, prefently.

Bid, pray for, defire.

Bledoch, butter milk.

Bowgil, a horn.

Brand, fword.

Bruke, poffefs, enjoy.

Binge, do obeyfance.

Bute, advantage.

Blutter, blunder.

Brecham, the collar of a
work horfe.

Bridal-renzie, a horfe's rein.

Browny, a kind of ghoft or
familiar fpirit.

C

CA'D about, put about.
Cadie, a cadet.

Cadgie, happy, chearful.

Can, 'gan, began.

Canker'd, angry, paffionately
fnarling.

Canna, cannot.

Cant, to tell merry old tales.

Cantrips, incantations.

Canty, chearful and merry.

Camftairie, riotous.

Capernoited, whimfical, ill-
natur'd, capricious.

Car, fledge.

Carnea, care not.

Carle, a name for an old
man.

Carline, an old woman.
Girecarline, a giant's
wife.

Cathel, an hot pot, made
of ale, fugar, and eggs.

Cauldrife. fpiritlefs. Wanting chearfulnefs in ad-
drefs.

Cauler, cool or frefh.

Cawk, chalk.

Call up, to upbraid.

Chafts, the chops.

Chandler, chandelier, a
candleftick.

Chapping, an ale-meafure
or ftoup, fomewhat lefs
than an Englifh quart.

Caſtocks, the core and ſtalk of cabbages.

Chiel, a general term, like fellow, uſed ſometimes with reſpect; as, He's a very good chiel; and contemptuouſly, as, That chiel.

Chirm, chirp and ſing like a bird.

Chitter, to ſhiver, to gnaſh the teeth.

Chucky, a hen.

Clan, tribe, family.

Clauk, a ſharp blow or ſtroke that makes a noiſe.

Claſhes, chat.

Clatter, chatter.

Claught, took hold.

Claver, to ſpeak nonſenſe.

Claw, ſcratch.

Claiſe, clothes.

Clead, to cloath.

Cleeding, cloathing.

Cleck, hatch.

Cleek, to catch as with a hook.

Cleugh, a den betwixt two rocks.

Clinty, hard, ſtony.

Clock, a beetle.

Clotted, the fall of any ſoft moiſt thing.

Cloſs, a court or ſquare; and frequently a lane or alley.

Clour, the little lump that riſes on the head, occaſioned by a blow or fall.

Clute or cloot, hoof of cows or ſheep.

Cockit, cocked.

Cockernony, the gathering of a woman's hair when it is wrapt or ſnooded up with a band or ſnood.

Cod, a pillow.

Coft, bought.

Cog, a pretty large wooden diſh the country people put their pottage in.

Cogle, when a thing moves backwards and forwards, inclining to fall.

Coodies, a ſmall wooden veſſel, uſed by ſome for chamber-pots.

Coof, a ſtupid fellow.

Coor, to cover.

Coot, the ankle.

Cooſer, a ſton'd horſe.

Cooſt, did caſt. Cooſten, thrown.

Corby, a raven.

Coſie, ſheltered in a convenient place.

Couter, the coulter of a plow.

Cotter, a ſubtenant.

Cowp, to fall; alſo a fall.

Cowp, to change, barter.

Cowp, a company of people; as, merry, ſenſeleſs, corky cowp.

Cour, to croutch and creep.

Couth, frank and kind.

Crack, to chat.

Craig, a rock.

Craig, neck.
Cog, a pail.
Creel, a basket.
Crish, greeze.
Croil, a crooked dwarf.
Croon or cruve, to murmur or hum over a song. The lowing of bulls.
Crouse, bold.
Crove, a little hutch or lodge.
Crove, a cottage.
Crummy, a cow's name.
Cryn, shrink or become less by drying.
Cryned, contracted, shrunk.
Cudeigh, a bribe, present.
Culzie, intice or flatter.
Cummers, gossips.
Cun, to taste, learn, know.
Cunzie or coonie, coin.
Curn, a small parcel.
Curssche, a kerchief. A linen dress, wore by our Highland women.
Cutled, used kind and gaining methods for obtaining love and friendship.
Cutts, lots. Thefe are usually made of straws unequally cut.
Cutty, short.

D.

DAB, a proficient.
Dad, to beat one thing against another. He fell wi' a dad. He dadded his head against the wall, &c.
Dad, a large piece.
Daddy, father.
Daft, foolish, and sometimes wanton.
Daffin, folly, waggery.
Dail or dale, a valley, a plain, a share.
Dainty, is used as an epithet of a fine man or woman.
Dander, wander to and fro, or faunter.
Dang, did ding, beat, thrust, drive. Ding dang, moving hastily one on tho back of another.
Danton, affright.
Darn, to hide.
Darna, dare not.
Dash, to put out of countenance.
Dawty, a fondling, darling. To dawt, to cocker; and carefs with tenderness.
Deary, little dear, a term of endearment.
Deave, to stun the ears with noise.
Dees, dairy maids.
Deray, merriment, jollity, solemnity, tumult, disorder, noise.
Dern, secret, hidden, lonely.
Deval, to descend, fall, hurry, desist.

Dight, checked, made ready; alfo to clean.

Dike, a wall.

Din, noife.

Dinna, do not.

Dings, excells.

Dirgie, a funeral feftival.

Dic'd, weaved in figures like dice.

Dirle, a fmarting pain quickly over.

Disjoin, breakfaft.

Dit, to ftop or clofe up a hole.

Divet, broad turf.

Docken, a dock (the herb).

Doilt, confufed and filly.

Doited, dozed or crazy, as in old age.

Doggie, a little dog.

Dole, a large piece, dole or fhare.

Donk, moift.

Donfie, affectedly neat. Clean, when applied to any little perfon.

Doofart, a dull heavy-headed fellow.

Dool, pain, grief.

Dorts, a proud pet.

Dorty, proud, not to be fpoke to, conceited, appearing as difobliged.

Dofen'd, cold, impotent.

Dought, could, avail'd.

Doughty, ftrong, valiant, and able.

Douks, dives under water.

Doufe, folid, grave, prudent.

Dow, to will, to incline, to thrive.

Dow, dove.

Dow'd (liquor) that's dead, or has loft the fpirits; or withered (plant).

Dowff, mournful, wanting vivacity.

Dowie, melancholy, fad, doleful.

Downa, dow not; i. e. tho' one has the power, he wants the heart to it.

Dowp, the arfe, the fmall remains of a candle, the bottom of an egg-fhell. *Better haff egg as toom dowp.*

Drammock and crowdie, meal kneaded with water.

Draff, brewers grains.

Draggled, draiket; dirtied, befpattered.

Drant, to fpeak flow, after a fighing manner.

Dree, to fuffer, endure.

Dreery, wearifome, frightful.

Dreigh, flow, keeping at a diftance. Hence an ill payer of his debts, we call, dreigh. Tedious.

Dribs, drops.

Drie, fuffer.

Drizel, a little water in a rivulet, fcarce appearing to run.

Droning, fitting lazily, or

moving heavily. Speaking with groans.

Drouked, drenched, all wet.

Drowket, drenched, draggled.

Dubs, mire.

Duds, duddies, rags, tattered garments.

Dulfe, fea-weed.

Dung, defeat.

Dunt, ftroke or blow.

Dunty, a doxy.

Durk, a poignard or dagger.

Dynles, trembles, fhakes.

Dyver, a bankrupt.

Endlang, along.

Erd, earth.

Ergh, fcrupulous, when one makes faint attempts to do a thing, without a fteady refolution.

Erft, time paft.

Eftler, hewn ftone. Buildings of fuch we call, eftler work.

Ether, an adder.

Ethercap, a wafp.

Ettle, to aim, defign.

Even'd, compar'd.

Fydent, diligent, laborious.

E

EAGS, incites, ftirs up.

Eam, uncle.

Eard, earth, the ground.

Earn, yern.

Edge (of a hill) is the fide or top.

Ee-brie, eye-brow.

Een, eyes.

Eild, age.

Eildens, of the fame age.

Eiftlin, eaftern.

Eith, eafy. Eithar, eafier.

Elbuck, elbow.

Elf-fhot, bewitched, fhot by fairies.

Elfon, a fhoemaker's awl.

Elritch, wild, hideous, uninhabited, except by imaginary ghofts.

Elwand, the meafure of an ell, or yard.

F

FA, a trap, fuch as is ufed for catching rats or mice.

Fae, a foe, an enemy.

Fadge, a fpungy fort of bread, in fhape of a roll.

Fag, to tire, or turn weary.

Fail, thick turf, fuch as are ufed for building dykes for folds, inclofures, &c.

Fain, expreffes earneft defire; as, Fain would I. Alfo, joyful, tickled with pleafure.

Fait, neat, in good order.

Fairfaw, when we wifh well to one, that a good or fair fate may befal him.

Fang, the talons of a fowl. To fang, to grip, or hold faft.

Farles, cakes.

Fafh, vex or trouble. Fafhious, troublefome.

Faugh, a colour between white and red. Faugh riggs, fallow ground.

Fauld, fence, inclofure.

Feck, a part, quantity; as, Maift feck, the greateft number; nae feck, very few.

Fecklefs, feeble, little, and weak.

Feed or fead, feud, hatred, quarrel.

Feint, the feint a bit, the never a bit.

Feinzie, feign.

Fen, fhift. Fending, living by induftry. Make a fen, fall upon methods.

Ferlie, wonder.

Fernzier, the laft or forerun year.

File, to defile or dirty.

Fire-fang'd, burnt.

Fireflaught, a flafh of lightning.

Fiftle, to ftir. A ftir.

Fitfted, the print of the foot.

Fizzing, whizzing.

Flae-lugged, q. d. he has a flea in his ear.

Flaffing, moving up and down, raifing wind by motion, as birds with their wings.

Flags, flafhes, as of wind and fire.

Flane, an arrow.

Flang, flung.

Flaughter, to pare turf from the ground.

Flaw, lie or fib.

Fleetch, to cox or flatter.

Fleg, fright.

Flewet, a fmart blow.

Fley or flie, to affright.

Fleyt, afraid or terrified.

Flighteren, fluttering.

Flinders, fplinters.

Flit, to remove.

Flite or flyte, to fcold, chide. Flet, did fcold.

Flowks, foal-fifh.

Flufhes, floods.

Fog, mofs.

Foordays, the morning far advanced, fair day-light.

Forby, befides.

Forebears, forefathers, anceftors.

Forfairn, abufed, befpattered.

Forfaughten, weary, faint, and out of breath with fighting.

Forgainft, oppofite to.

Forgether, to meet, encounter.

Forleet, to forfake or forget.

Foreftam, the forehead.

Fouth, abundance, plenty.

Fow, full, drunk.

Fozy, fpungy, foft.

Frais, to make a noife. We ufe to fay, One makes a frais, when they boaft, wonder, and talk more of a matter than it is worthy of, or will bear.

Fray, buftle, fighting.

Freik, a fool, light, impertinent fellow.

Fremit, ftrange, not-a-kin.

Frifted, trufted.

Frufh, brittle, like bread baken with butter.

Fudgel, plump.

Fudder, 128 lb. put for any large quantity.

Fuff, to blow. Fuffin, blowing.

Furder, profper.

Furlot, a meafure, beingthe 4th of a boll.

Furthy, forward.

Fufh, brought.

Furlet, four pecks.

Fute braid fawing, corn to fow a foot-breadth.

Fyk, to be reftlefs, uneafy.

G

G AB, the mouth. To prat. *Gab fae gafh.*

Gabbing, pratting pertly. To give faucy returns when reprimanded.

Gabbocks, large mouthfuls.

Gabby, one of a ready and eafy expreffion; the fame with Auld-gabbet.

Gaberlunzie, a beggar's wallet.

Gaed, went.

Gafaw, a hearty loud laughter. To gawf, laugh.

Gait, a goat.

Gains, gums.

Gang, go.

Gar, to caufe, make, or force.

Gare, greedy, rapacious, earneft to have a thing.

Gafh, folid, fagacious. One with a long out-chin, we call, Gafh-gabbet, Gafhbeard.

Gate, way.

Gaunt, yawn.

Gawky, idle, ftaring, idiotical perfon.

Gawn, going.

Gaws, galls.

Gawfy, jolly, buxom.

Gear, wealth, goods.

Geck, to mock, to loath.

Geed or gade, went.

Genty, handfome, genteel,

Gerfons, fines paid by tenants.

Get or brat, a child, by way of contempt or derifion.

Ghaift, ghoft.

Gif, if.

Giglet, gilflirt.

Gillygacus or gillygapus, a ftaring, gaping fool; a gormandizer.

Gilpy, a roguifh boy

Gimmer, a young fheep(ew).

Gin, if.

Gird, to ftrike, pierce.

Girdle, an iron-plate for toafting oat-bread.

Girn, to grin, fnarl; alfo a fnare or trap, fuch as boys make of horfe-hair to catch birds.

Girth, a hoop.

Glaiks, an idle good-for-nothing fellow. Glaiked, foolifh, wanton, light. To give the glaiks, to beguile one, by giving him his labour for his pains.

Glaifter, to bawl or bark.

Glamour, fafcination. When devils, wizards, or jugglers deceive the fight, they are faid, to caft glamour over the eyes of the fpectator.

Glar, mire, oozy matter.

Gled, kite.

Glee, to fquint.

Glee, mirth.

Gleg, fharp, quick, active.

Glen, a narrow valley between mountains.

Glengore, the foul difeafe.

Glib, fmooth, fliding.

Gloom, to fcoul or frown.

Glowming, the twilight, or evening-gloom.

Glowr, to ftare, look ftern.

Glumfh, to hang the brow, and grumble.

Goolie, a large knife.

Goofhet, the clock of a ftocking.

Gorlings or gorblings, young unfledged birds.

Goffie, goffip.

Gove, to look broad and ftedfaft, holding up the face.

Gewans, daifies.

Gowden, golden.

Gowf, befides the known game, a racket or found blow on the chops, we call a Gowf on the haffet.

Grape, a ftable-rake.

Gutcher, grandfather.

Gouk, the cuckow. In derifion, we call a thoughtlefs fellow, and one who harps too long on one fubject, a gowk.

Gowl, a howling, to bellow and cry.

Goufty, ghaftly, large, wafte, defolate, and frightful.

Grany, grandmother, any old woman.

Grane, to groan.

Grape, a trident fork; alfo to grope.

Gravy, fauce.

Gree, prize, victory.

Green, to long for.

Greet, to weep. Grat, wept.

Grieve, an overfeer.

Grip, to hold faft.

Groff, grofs, coarfe.

Grotts, mill'd oats.

Grouf, to lie flat on the belly.

Grounche or glunſhe, to grudge.

Grutten, wept.

Grit, great.

Gryſe, a pig.

Gumption, good ſenſe.

Gurly, rough, bitter, cold (weather.)

Grunzie, ſnout.

Geſened, when the wood of any veſſel is ſhrunk with dryneſs.

Gytlings, young children.

Guſty, ſavoury.

Graith all kinds of inſtruments.

H

HAffet, the cheek, ſide of the head.

Hawick gill. A gill is a meaſure for ſpirits, containing half a pint. A Hawick gill is a double gill, ſo named from the town of Hawick.

Hoſe, ſtockings.

Halucket, crazy.

Haddock, a ſmall fiſh.

Hinny, honey.

Hald, dwelling, tenement.

Hodling, hobling.

Hafs-bane, breaſt-bone.

Haf-mark bridal - band, clandeſtine marriage.

Hap, covering.

Heartſome, gladſome, pleaſant.

Hawſlock, wool next the windpipe.

Haith, in faith.

Heh! hah!

Heffs, lodges.

Hawkies, cows.

Halflin, partly.

Hool, the ſhell.

Holden-gray, a coarſe gray cloth.

Hap, cover.

Herried, plundered.

Hubbilſchow, confuſion, uproar.

Hide, ſkin.

Heck, a rack.

Hog, a ſheep of two years old.

Hoble ſhoon, clouted ſhoes.

Hagabag, coarſe table linen.

Haggiſe, a kind of pudding made of the lungs and liver of a ſheep, and boiled in the ſtomack bag.

Hags, hacks, peat-pits, or breaks in moſſy ground.

Hain, to ſave, manage narrowly.

Haleſome, wholeſome.

Hale, whole.

Halanſhakers, ragamuffins.

Hameld, domeſtic.

Hamely, friendly, frank, open, kind.

Hanty, convenient, handſome.

Harle, drag.

Harns, brains. Harn-pan, the ſcull.

Harfhip, ruin.

Haufe, to embrace.

Hafh, a floven.

Haveren or havrel, id.

Haughs, valleys, or low grounds on the fides of rivers.

Heal or heel, health, or whole.

Heeryeftreen, the night before yefternight.

Heez, to lift up a heavy thing a little. A heezy is a good lift.

Heft, handle.

Heftit, accuftomed to live in a place.

Heght, promifed; alfo named.

Hempy, a tricky wag, fuch for whom the hemp grows.

Hereit, ruined in eftate, broke, fpoiled.

Hefp, a clafp or hook, bar, or bolt; alfo, in yarn, a certain number of threads.

Hether-bells, the heath-bloffom.

Heugh, a rock or fteep hill; alfo, a coal-pit.

Hiddils or hidliugs, lurking, hiding places. To do a thing in hidlings, i. e. privately.

Hirple, to move flowly and lamely.

Hirfle, or hirdfale, a flock of cattle.

Ho, a fingle ftocking.

Hobblefhew, a confufed rout, noife.

Hool, hufk. Hool'd, inlofed.

Hooly, flow.

Hoft or whoft, to cough.

How or hu, a cap or roof-tree.

How, low ground, a hollow.

How! ho!

Howdered, hidden.

Howdy, midwife.

Howk, to dig.

Howns, plains, or river-fides.

Howt! fy!

Howtowdy, a young hen.

Hnrkle, to crouch, or bow together like a cat, hedge-hog, or hare.

Hurl-barrow, a wheel-barrow.

Hut, a hovel.

Hyt, mad.

J

JACK, jacket.

Jog, to prick as with a pin.

Jaw, a wave or gufh of water.

Icefhogles, icicles.

Jee, to incline to one fide. To jee back and fore, is to move like a balance up and down, to this and the other fide.

Jig, to crack, make a noise like a cart-wheel.

Jimp, slender.

Jip, gypsie.

Ilk, each. Ilka, every.

In-kneed, crook-kneed.

Jow, the toll of a bell.

Ingan, onion.

Ingle, fire.

Jo, sweetheart.

Jowk, a low bow.

Irie, fearful, terrified, as if afraid of some ghost or apparition. Also, melancholy.

I'se, I shall.

I'll, I will.

Isles, embers.

Junt, a large joint or piece of meat.

Jute, sour or dead liquor.

Jupe, to mock. Gibe, taunt.

Ill-far'd, ugly.

Jack, a piece of armour.

K

Kale or kail, colewort, and sometimes broth.

Kacky, to dung.

Kain, a part of a farm-rent paid in fowls.

Kame, comb.

Kanny or conny, fortunate; also wary, one who manages his affairs discreetly.

Kebbuck, a cheese.

Keckle, to laugh, to be noisy.

Kedgy, jovial.

Keel, red chalk.

Keek, to peep.

Kelt, cloth with a freeze; commonly made of native black wool.

Kemp, to strive who shall perform most of the same work in the same time.

Ken, to know; used in England as a noun. A thing within ken, i. e. within view.

Kent, a long staff, such as shepherds use for leaping over ditches.

Kepp, to catch a thing that moves towards one.

Kith, and kin, kindred.

Kiest, did cast. Vid. Coost.

Kilted, tuck'd up.

Kimmer, a female gossip.

Kirn, a churn, to churn.

Kist, chest.

Kirtle, an upper petticoat.

Kitchen, all sorts of eatables except bread.

Kit, a wooden vessel, hooped and staved.

Kittle, difficult, mysterious, obscure (writings.)

Kittle, to tickle, ticklish.

Knacky, witty and facetious.

Knoit, to beat or strike sharply.

Knoos'd, buffeted and bruised.

Knoost or knuist, a large lump.

Know, a hillock.

Knockit, beat, bruised.

Knublock, a knob.

Knuckies, only used in Scotch for the finges next the back of the hand.

Kow, goblin, or any person one stands in awe to disoblige, and fears.

Ky, kine or cows.

Kyth, to appear. He'll kyth in his ain colours.

Kyte, the belly.

Kurches, a covering for the neck.

L

Laggert, bespattered, covered with clay.

Laigh, low.

Laith, loath, sorry.

Lane, my lane, by myself.

Late-wake, a sort of festival at watching a corpse.

Laird, a gentleman of estate.

Lack, want.

Lak or lack, undervalue, contemn; as, He that laks my mare, would buy my mare.

Landart, the country, or belonging to it. Rustic.

Lane, alone.

Langour, languishing, melancholy. To hold one out of langour, i. e. to divert him.

Langsome, tiresome, tedious.

Langkale, coleworts uncut.

Lap, leaped.

Lapper'd, curdled or clotted.

Lare, a place for laying, or that has been lain in.

Lare, bog.

Lair, learning.

Lave, the rest or remainder.

Lawin, a tavern reckoning.

Lawland, low country.

Lavrock, the lark.

Lawty or lawtith, justice, fidelity, honesty.

Leal, true, upright, honest, faithful to truit, loyal. A leal heart never lied.

Leam, flame.

Lear, learning, to learn.

Lee, untilled ground; also, an open grassy plain, leez.

Leglen, a milking-pail with one lug or handle.

Leman, a lover.

Lemmane, a mistress.

Leugh, laughed.

Lew-warm, lukewarm.

Libbit, gelded.

Lick, to whip or beat; item, a wag or cheat, we call a great lick.

Lied, ye lied, ye tell a lie.

Lift, the sky or firmament.

Liggs, lyes.

Lilts, the holes of a wind inftrument of mufick; hence, Lilt up a fpring. Lilt it out, take off your drink merrily.

Limmer, a whore.

Limp, to halt.

Lin, a cataract.

Ling, quick career in a ſtraight line, to gallop.

Lingle, cord, ſhoemakers. threed.

Linkan, walking fpeedily.

Lintwhites, linnets.

Lint-tap, lint on the diſtaff.

Lang-fyne, long ago.

Let, hinderance.

Lire, breaſts; item, the moſt muſcular parts; fometimes the air or complection of the face.

Lirk, a wrinkle or fold.

Liſk, the flank.

Lith, a joint.

Loan, a little common near to country villages, where they milk their cows.

Loch, a lake.

Loo, to love, or lue.

Loof, the hollow of the hand.

Looms, tools, inſtruments in general, veſſels.

Loot, did let

Low, flame.

Lowan, flaming.

Lown, calm. Keep lown, be fecret.

Loun, rogue, whore, villain.

Lounder, a found blow.

Lout, to bow down, making courtefy. To ſtoop.

Luck, to inclofe, ſhut up, faſten. Hence Lucken-handed, clofe-fiſted; Lucken Gowns, Booths, &c.

Lucky, grandmother or goody.

Lug, ear. Handle of a pot or veſſel.

Luggie, a diſh of wood with a handle.

Lum, the chimney.

Lure, rather.

Lurdan, lazy fot.

Lyart, hoary, or grey-hair'd.

M

MAik or make, match, equal.

Maiklefs, matchlefs.

Mailen, a farm.

Makly, feemly, well-proportioned.

Makſna, it is no matter.

Malifon, a curfe, malediction.

Mangit, gall'd or bruifed by toil or ſtripes.

Manfworn, perjured.

Mantile, a lady's mantle or cloak.

Mank, a want.

March or merch, a landmark, border of lands.

Mavis, thruſh.

Marrow, mate, lover.

Muck, dung

Meikle, much, great.

Mou, mouth.

Monſmeg, a very large ancient piece of ordnance, ſo called, which was lately tranſported from the caſtle of Edinburgh to the tower of London. It was of an enormous bore; and if we rightly remember was formed of pieces of iron, fitted together length-ways, and hooped with iron rings; this being the plan of all the firſt pieces of artillery, which ſucceeding the battering engines of the ancients, were employed, like theſe, in throwing ſtones of a prodigious weight.

Meal-kail, ſoup with pot-herbs and meal.

Mill, a ſnuff-box.

Mawn, mown.

Mittens, worſted gloves.

Munandy, monday.

Mottie, ſpotted, defiled.

Miſluck, misfortunes.

Minnin, minnow.

Maries, waiting-maids.

Maiſter, piſs.

Marrow, mate, fellow, equal, comrade.

Maſk, to maſh, in brewing. Maſking-loom, maſh-vat.

Maun, muſt. Mauna, muſt not, may not,

Meikle, much, big, great, large.

Meith, limit, mark, ſign.

Mends, ſatisfaction, revenge, retaliation. To make amends, to make a grateful return.

Menſe, diſcretion, ſobriety, good-breeding. Menſfou, mannerly.

Menzie, company of men, army, aſſembly, one's followers.

Meſſen, a little dog, lap-dog.

Mell, a mallet.

Midding, a dunghill.

Midges, gnats, little flies.

Mim, affectedly modeſt.

Mint, aim, endeavour.

Mirk, dark.

Milk-ſyth, milk-ſtrainer.

Minny, mother.

Miſcaw, to give names.

Miſchance, misfortune.

Miſken, to neglect, or not take notice of one; alſo, let alone.

Miſluſhous, malicious, rough.

Miſters, neceſſities, wants.

Mony, many.

Mools, the earth of the grave.

Mool, to crumble. To mool in, to partake.

Moup, to eat, generally uſed of children, or of old

people, who have but few teeth, and make their lips move faſt, though they eat but ſlow.

Mow, a pile or bing, as of feuel, hay, ſheaves of corn, &c.

Mows, jeſts.

Muckle, ſee Meikle.

Murgullied miſmanaged, a-buſed.

Mutch, coif.

Mutchken, an Engliſh pint.

N

NAcky or knacky, clever, active in ſmall affairs.

Naſay, denial.

Neeſe, noſe.

Nettle, to fret or vex.

Newfangle, fond of a new thing.

New-mawn, new-mow'd.

Nevel, a found blow with the fiſt.

Nick, to bite or cheat. Nicked, cheated: alſo, as a cant word to drink heartily.; as, He nicks fine.

Nieſt, next.

Niffer, to exchange or bar-ter.

Niffnafan, trifling.

Nignays, trifles.

Nips, bits.

Nither, to ſtraiten. Ni-thered, hungered, or half-ſtarved in main-tenance.

Nive, the fiſt.

Nivefow, a handful.

Nock, notch or nick of an arrow or ſpindle.

Noit, ſee Knoit.

Nook, corner.

Nor, than.

Nowt, cows, kine.

Nowther, neither.

Nuckle, new calv'd (cows).

O

OE, a grandchild. O'er or ower, too much; as, A' o'ers is vice, All exceſs is vicious.

O'ercome, ſuperplus.

O'erput, to overcome.

Ony, any.

Or, ſometimes uſed for ere, or before. Or day, i. e. before day-break.

Ora, any thing over what's needful.

Orp, to weep with a con-vulſive pant.

Oughtlens, in the leaſt.

Owk, week.

Ourlay, a cravat.

Owſen, oxen.

Owther, either.

Oxter, the arm-pit.

P

PACE, eaſter. Paddock, a frog.

Paddock-ride, the fpawn of frogs.

Padell, a fhovel.

Paiks, chaftifement. To paik, to beat or belabour one foundly.

Pang, to fqueeze, prefs, or pack one thing into another.

Pap, breaft. Take the pap, take the breaft.

Partans, crab-fifh.

Paughty, proud, haughty.

Paunches, tripe.

Pawky, witty, or fly in word or action, without any harm or bad defigns.

Pearlings, lace of threed.

Peck, the 16th of a boll.

Peer, a key or wharf.

Peets, turf for fire.

Pegh, to pant.

Penfand, thinking.

Penfy, finical, foppifh, conceited.

Perfyte, perfect.

Perquire, by heart.

Pett, a favourite, a fondling. To pettle, to dandle, feed, cherifh, flatter. Hence, to take the pett, is to be peevifh or fullen, as commonly petts are when in the leaft difobliged.

Pettled, fondled, pampered.

Pibroughs, fuch Highland tunes as are played on bag-pipes before them when they go out to battle.

Pig, an earthen pitcher.

Pike, to pick out, or chufe.

Pillar, the ftool of repentance.

Pimpin, pimping, mean, fcurvy.

Pine, pain or pining.

Pingle, to contend, ftrive, or work hard.

Pirn, the fpool or quill within the fhuttle, which receives the yarn. Pirny (cloth) or a web of unequal threads or colours, ftripped.

Pith, ftrength, might, force.

Plack, two bodles, or the third of a penny Englifh.

Plaid, ftripped, woolen covering.

Pleen, complain.

Pleugh, plow.

Plucky-faced, pimpled.

Poortith, poverty.

Pople or paple, the bubbling, purling, or boiling up of water.

Porridge, pottage.

Pouch, a pocket.

Pow, fkull.

Powny, a little horfe or galloway; alfo, a turky.

Powfowdie, ram-head foup.

Pratick, practice, art, ftratagem. Priving pratick, trying ridiculous experiments.

Prets, tricks, rogueries. We say, He plaid me a pret, *i. e.* cheated. The callan's fou o' prets, *i. e.* has abundance of waggish tricks.

Prig, to cheapen, or importune for a lower price of goods one is buying.

Prin, a pin.

Prive, prie, to prove or taste.

Propine, gift or prefent.

Pryme or prime, to fill or stuff.

Putt a stane, throw a big stone.

Q

QUAT, quit.
Quey, a young cow.
Quhittill, knife.

R

RAcket, blow, box on the ear.

Racklefs, carelefs; one who does things without regarding whether they be good or bad, we call him Racklefs handed.

Rae, a roe.

Raffan, merry, roving, hearty.

Raird, a loud found.

Rair, roar.

Rak or rook, a mist or fog.

Rampage, to fpeak and act furioufly.

Ranting, roufing, jolly.

Rape, rope.

Raihes, ruihes.

Ratch, hound.

Rave, did rive or tear.*

Raught, reached.

Rax, to ftretch. Rax'd, reached.

Ream, cream. Whence reaming; as, reaming liquor.

Red up, drefs adjufted.

Red-wood, mad, furious.

Redd, to rid, unravel. To feparate folks that are fighting. It alfo fignifies clearing of any paffage. I'm redd, I'm apprehenfive.

Rede, counfel, advice; as, I wad na rede ye do that.

Reek, reach; alfo, fmoke.

Reeft, to ruft, or dry in the fmoke.

Reft, bereft, robbed, forced or carried away.

Reif, rapine, robbery.

Reik or rink, a courfe or race.

Reveled, entangled.

Rever, a robber or pirate.

Rew, to repent.

Rewth. pity.

Rice or rife, bulruihes, bramble-branches, or twigs of trees.

Rifarts, raddifhes.

Rife or ryfe, plenty.

Rift, to belch.

Rigs, ridges.

Rigging, the back or rig-back, the top or ridge of a houfe.

Ripples, a weaknefs in the back and reins.

Ripling-kame, a comb for dreffing flax.

Rive, to rend, fplit, or burft.

Rock, a diftaff.

Rood, the crofs.

Roofe or rufe, to commend, extol.

Roove, to rivet.

Rottan, a rat.

Roudes, a term of reproach for an old woman.

Roundel, a witty, and often a fatyric kind of rhime.

Rowan, rolling.

Rowfted, grown ftiff, or rufty.

Rowt, to roar, efpecially the lowing of bulls and cows.

Rowth, plenty.

Ruck, a rick or ftack of hay or corns.

Rude, the red taint of the complection.

Ruefu, doleful.

Rug, to pull, take away by force.

Rumple, the rump.

Rungs, fmall boughs of trees, lopped off.

Runkle, a wrinkle.

Runckle, to ruffle.

S

Saebeins, feeing it is. Since.

Saiklefs, guiltlefs, free, forfaken, friendlefs.

Sall, fhall. Like foud for fhould.

Samen, the fame.

Sand-blird, pur-blind, fhort-fighted.

Sappy, moift, liquorifh.

Sark, a fhirt.

Saugh, a willow or fallow-tree.

Saw, an old faying, or proverbial expreffion.

Scad, fcald.

Scant, fcarce, fmall. Scanty tocher, fmall portion.

Scar, the bare places on the fides of hills wafhed down with rain.

Scart, to fcratch.

Scawp, a bare dry piece of ftony ground,

Scon, a cake of bread.

Scouling, frowning.

Scowp, to leap or move haftily from one place to another.

Scowth, room, freedom.

Scrimp, narrow, ftraitened, little.

Scroggs, fhrubs, thorns, briers.

Scroggy, thorny.

Scuds, ale. A late name gi-
ven it by the benders.

Scunner, to loath.

Sell, felf.

Serf, vaffal, fervant.

Seuch, furrow, ditch.

Sey, to try.

Seybow, a young onion.

Shaggy, crooked, wry.

Shan, pitiful, filly, poor.

Shanks, limbs.

Shanks-naigie, on foot.

Sharn, cow's dung.

Shave, a flice.

Shaw, a wood or foreft.

Shawl, fhallow.

Shawn, fhewn.

Shawps, empty hufks.

Sheen, fhining.

Shield, a fhed.

Shill, fhrill, having a fharp
found.

Shin, the ancle.

Shire, clear, thin. We call
thin cloth, or clear liquor,
fhire ; alfo, a clever wag,
a fhire lick.

Shog, to wag, fhake, or
jog backwards and for-
wards.

Shool, fhovel.

Shoon, fhoes.

Shore, to threaten, to cut.

Shottle, a drawer.

Sib, a-kin.

Sic, fuch.

Sicken, fuch.

Sicker, firm, fecure.

Sike, a rill or rivulet, commonly dry in fummer.

Siller, filver.

Sindle or finle, feldom.

Singit, finged.

Sinfyne, fince that time.
Lang fynfyne, long ago.

Skaill, to fcatter.

Skair, fhare.

Skaith, hurt, damage.

Skeigh, fkittifh.

Skelf, fhelf.

Skelp, to run. Ufed when
one runs barefoot. Alfo,
a fmall fplinter of wood.
Item, To flog the hips.

Skiff, to move fmoothly away.

Skink, a kind of ftrong
broth, made of cows
hams or knuckles; alfo,
to fill drink in a cup.

Skip, leap.

Skipper, pilot.

Skirl, to fhriek or cry with
a fhrill voice.

Sklate, flate. Skailie, is a
fine blue flate.

Skowrie, ragged, nafty, idle.

Skreed, a rent.

Skybauld, a tatterdemalion.

Skyt, fly out haftily.

Slade or flaid, did flide, mo-
ved, or made a thing
move eafily.

Slap or flak, a gap or narrow pafs between two
hills. Slap, a breach
in a wall.

Slavering, drivelling or flob-
bering.

Sled, fledge.

Slee, fly.

Sleek, fmooth.

Sleet, a fhower of half-melted fnow.

Slerg, to bedawb or plaifter.

Slid, fmooth, cunning, flippery; as, He's a flid lown. Slippy, flippery.

Slippery, fleepy.

Slonk, a mire, ditch, or flough; to wade throw a mire.

Slote, a bar or bolt for a door.

Slough, hufk or coat.

Smaik, a filly little pitiful fellow; the fame with fmatchet.

Smirky, fmiling.

Smittle, infectious or catching.

Smoor, to fmother.

Snack, nimble, ready, clever.

Snaw-ba's, jokes, farcafms.

Sneeft, an air of difdain.

Sned, to cut.

Sneer, to laugh in derifion.

Sneg, to cut; as Sneg'd off at the web's end.

Snell, fharp, fmarting, bitter, firm.

Snib, fnub, check, or reprove, correct.

Snifter, to fnuff or breathe through the nofe a little ftopt.

Snod, metaphorically ufed for neat, handfome, tight.

Snood, the band for tying up a woman's hair.

Snool, to difpirit by chiding, hard labour, and the like; alfo, a pitiful groveling flave.

Snoove, to whirl round.

Snotter, fnot.

Snout, nofe.

Snurl, to ruffle, wrinkle.

Snut, to curl the nofe in difdain.

Sod, a thick turf.

Sonfy, happy, fortunate, lucky: fometimes ufed for large and lufty.

Sore, forrel, reddifh-coloured.

Sorn, to fpunge.

Sofs, the noife that a thing makes when it falls to the ground.

Sough, the found of wind amongft trees, or of one fleeping.

Sowens, flummery, or oatmeal fowr'd amongft water for fome time, then boiled to a confiftency, and eaten with milk or butter.

Sowf, to conn over a tune on an inftrument.

Sowm, a fcore of fheep.

Spae, to foretel or divine. Spaemen, prophets, augurs.

Spain, to wean from the breaft.

Spait, a torrent, flood, or inundation.

Spaldings, fmall fifh dried and falted.

Spang, a jump; to leap or jump.

Spaul, fhoulder, arm.

Speel, to climb.

Speer, to afk, enquire.

Spelder, to fplit, ftretch, draw afunder.

Spence, the place of the houfe where provifions are kept.

Spice, pride.

Spill, to fpoil, abufe.

Spindle and whorl, inftruments pertaining to a diftaff.

Spoolie, fpoil, booty, plunder.

Spraings, ftripes of different colours.

Spring, a tune on a mufical inftrument.

Sprufh, fpruce.

Spruttl'd, fpeckled, fpotted.

Spung, purfe.

Spunk, tinder.

Spurtle, a flat iron for turning cakes.

Staig, a young horfe.

Stalwart, ftrong and valiant.

Stang, did fting; alfo, a fting or pole.

Stank, a pool of ftanding water.

Sow-libber, fow-gelder.

Stark, ftrong, robuft.

Starns, the ftars. Starn, a fmall moiety. We fay, Ne'er a ftarn.

Stay, fteep; as. Set, a ftout heart to a ftay brae.

Steek, to fhut, clofe.

Stegh, to cram.

Stend or ften, to move with a hafty long pace.

Stent, to ftretch or extend, to tax.

Stick out, juts out.

Stipend, a benefice.

Stint, to confine.

Stirk, a fteer or bullock.

Stoit or ftot, to rebound or reflect.

Stoar, rough, horfe.

Stool, a feat. The ftool of repentance is a confpicuous feat in the Prefbyterian churches, where thofe perfons who have been guilty of incontinence are obliged to appear before the congregation for feveral fuccefsive Sundays, and receive a public rebuke from the minifter.

Stou, to cut or crop. A ftou, a large cut or piece.

Stound, a fmarting pain or ftit h.

Stoup, a can.

Soup, a drop, a quantity liquid.

GLOSSARY. 269

Stour, duft agitated by winds, men or horfe feet. To ftour, to run quickly.

Stowth, ftealth.

Strapan, clever, tall, handfome.

Strath, a plain on a river fide.

Streek, to ftretch.

Striddle, to ftride; applied commonly to one that's little.

Strinkle, to fprinkle or ftraw.

Stroot or ftrut, ftuff'd full, drunk.

Strunt, a pet. To take the ftrunt, to be petted or out of humour.

Studdy, an anvil, or fmith's ftithy.

Sturdy, giddy-headed; *item*, ftrong.

Sture or ftoor, ftiff, ftrong, hoarfe.

Sturt, trouble, difturbance, vexation

Stym, a blink, or a little fight of a thing.

Suddle, to fully or defile.

Snmph, blockhead.

Sunkan, fplenetic.

Sunkots, fomething.

Sutor, fhoemaker.

Swaird, the furface of the grafs.

Swak, to throw, caft with force.

Swankies, clever young fellows.

Swarf, to fwoon away.

Swap, to exchange.

Swafh, fquat, fuddled.

Swatch, a pattern.

Swats, fmall ale.

Swecht, burden, weight, force.

Sweer, lazy, flow.

Sweeties, confections.

Swelt, fuffocated, choaked to death.

Swith, begone quickly.

Swinger, ftout wencher.

Swither, to be doubtful whether to do this or that.

Sybows, a fpecies of fmall onions.

Syne, afterwards, then.

T

TACKEL, an arrow.

Taid, toad.

Tane, taken,

Tane, the one.

Taiken, token.

Tangles, fea-weed.

Tap, a head. Such a quantity of lint as fpinfters put upon the diftaff, is called a Lint-tap.

Tape, to ufe any thing fparingly.

Z 2

Tappit-hen, the Scotch quart ftoup.

Tarrow, to refufe what we love, from a crofs humour.

Tartan, crofs ftripped ftuff of various colours, checkered, The Highland plaid.

Tafs, a little dram-cup.

Tate, a fmall lock of hair; or any little quantity of wool, cotton, &c.

Taunt to mock.

Tawpy, a foolifh wench.

Taz, a whip or fcourge.

Ted, to fcatter, fpread.

Tee, a little earth, on which gamefters at the gowf fet their balls before they ftrike them off.

Teen or Tynd, anger, rage, forrow.

Tenfome, the number of ten.

Tent, attention. Tenty, cautious.

Teugh, tough.

Thack, thatch. Thacker, thatcher.

Thae, thofe.

Tharms, fmall tripes.

Theek, to thatch.

Thir, thefe.

Thirled, bound, engaged.

Thole, to endure, fuffer.

Thoufe, thou fhalt.

Thow, thaw.

Thowlefs, unactive, filly, lazy, heavy.

Thraw-crook, a crooked

ftick for twifting hay or ftraw ropes.

Thrawart, froward, crofs, crabbed.

Thrawin, ftern and crofs-grained.

Threep, to aver, alledge, urge, and affirm boldly.

Thud, a blaft, blow, ftorm, or the violent found of thefe. Cry'd, heh at ilka thud; i. e. gave a groan at every blow.

Tid, tide or time; proper time; as, He took the tid.

Tift, good order, health.

Tight, neat.

Tine, to lofe. Tint, loft.

Tike, dog.

Tinkler, tinker.

Tinfel, lofs.

Tip, or tippony, ale fold for 2 d. the Scotch pint.

Tirl at the pin, rap with the knocker.

Tirl or tir, to uncover a houfe, or undrefs a perfon; ftrip one naked. Sometimes a fhort action is named a Tirle; as, They took a tirle of dancing, drinking, &c.

Titty, fifter.

Tocher, portion, dowry.

Tod, a fox.

Todling, reeling, tottering.

Tooly, to fight. A fight or quarrel.

Toom, empty; applied to

a barrel, purſe, houſe, &c. *Item*, to empty.

Toſh, tight, neat.

Tovy, warm, pleaſant, half fuddled.

To the fore, in being, alive, unconſumed.

Touſe or touzle, to rumple, teaze.

Tout, the ſound of a horn or trumpet.

Tow, a rope, A Tyburn neck-lace, or St Johnſtoun ribband.

Towmond, a year or twelve-month.

Trewes, hoſe and breeches all of a piece.

Trig, neat, handſome.

Troke, exchange.

True, to true, truſt, be-lieve; as, *True ye fae?* or *Love gars me true ye:*

Trencher, wooden platter.

Tryſt, appointment.

Twin, to part with, to ſe-parate from.

Twitch, touch.

Twinters, ſheep of two years old.

Tydie, plump, fat, lucky.

Tynd, *vide* Teen.

Tyſt, to entice, ſtir up, al-lure.

U.

UGG, to deteſt, hate, nau-feate.

Ugſome, hateful, nauſeous, horrible.

Umwhile, the late, or de-ceaſed, ſome time ago. Of old.

Undocht or wandocht, a ſilly, weak perſon.

Uneith, not eaſy.

Ungeard, naked, not clad, unharneſſed.

Unko or unco, uncouth, ſtrange.

Unlooſome, unlovely.

Vougy, elevated, proud. That boaſts or brags of any thing.

W.

WAD or wed, pledge, wager, pawn; alſo, would.

Waff, wandering by itſelf.

Wak, moiſt, wet.

Wakrife, wakeful.

Waladay! alas! welloday!

Wale, to pick and chuſe. The wale, *i. e.* the beſt.

Wallets, bags.

Wallop, to move ſwiftly, with much agitation.

Wally, choſen, beautiful, large. A bonny wally, *i. e.* a fine thing.

Wame, womb.

Wamill, ſtomach turns.

Wandought, want of dought, impotent.

Waneafe, uneafinefs.

Wangrace, wickednefs, want of grace.

Wap, a fudden ftroke.

War, worfe.

Ware, goods, to fpend.

Warlock, wizard.

Wat or wit, to know.

Waught, a large draught.

Waughts, drinks largely.

Wearifu', woeful.

Wee, little ; as, A wanton wee thing.

Wean or wee ane, a child.

Ween, thought, imagined, fuppofed.

Weer, to ftop or oppofe.

Weir, war.

Weird, fate or deftiny.

Weit, rain.

Werfh, infipid, wallowifh, wanting falt.

Weftlin, weftern.

Whang, a large portion of any thing.

Whauk, whip, beat, flog.

Whid, to fly quickly. A whid is a hafty flight.

Whilk, which.

Whilly, to cheat. Whilly-wha, a cheat.

Whinging, whining, fpeaking with a doleful tone.

Whinger, hanger.

Whins, furze.

Whifht, hufht. Hold your peace.

Whilk, to pull out haftily.

Whomilt, turned upfide-down.

Wight, ftout, clever, active, item, a man or perfon.

Wilks, perriwinkles.

Wimpling, a turning backward and foreward, winding like the meanders of a river.

Win or won, to refide, dwell.

Winna, will not.

Winnocks, windows.

Winfom, gaining, defirable, agreeable, complete, large ; we fay, My winfome love.

Wirrykow, a bugbear.

Wifent, parched, dry, withered.

Wiftle, to exchange (money.)

Witherfhins, crofs motion, or againft the fun.

Won, to refide, to dwell.

Woo or W, wool; as in the whim of making five words out of four letters, thus, z, a, e, w; (i. e.) Is it all one wool?

Wood, mad.

Woody, the gallows.

Wordy, worthy.

Wow! ftrange! wonderful!

Wrath, a fpirit, or phantom.

Wreaths (of fnow), when

heaps of it are blown to-
gether by the wind.

Wyfing, inclining. To wyfe,
to lead, train.

Wyfon, the gullet.

Wyte, to blame. Blame.

Y

YAMPH, to bark, or
make a noife like little
dogs.

Yap, hungry, having a long-
ing defire for any thing.

Yamers, a cry of fowls, as,
ca, ca.

Yealtou, yea wilt thou.

Yed, to contend, wrangle.

Yeld, barren, as a cow
that gives no milk.

Yerk, to do any thing with
celerity.

Yerd, earth.

Yefk, the hiccup.

Yett, gate.

Yeftreen, yefternight.

Yied, went.

Youdith, youthfulnefs.

Yowden, wearied.

Yowls, howlings, fcreams.

Yowf, a fwinging blow.

Yuke, the itch.

Yule, Chriftmas.

I N D E X.

N. B. The Figures refer to the Page, and the
Numerals to the Volume.

A

ABOUT zule whan the wind blew cule,   i 17

  As Bothwel was walking in the Highlands

    alone,   i 83

As it fell out on a long summer's day,   i 85

As I was walking all alone,   i 95

A' the boys of merry Linkim,   i 96

A better mason than Lammikin,   i 145

An thou wert mine ain thing,   i 171

Awake, my love, with genial ray,   i 188

As I came in by Tiviot-side,   i 201

Adieu, ye streams that smoothly glide,   i 215

Ah, Chloris, could I now but sit,   i 219

Ah, the shepherd's mournful fate,   i 220

Adieu for a while, my native green plains,   i 242

As walking forth to view the plain,   i 245

As I went forth to view the spring,   i 265

As Sylvia in a forest lay,   i 270

As from a rock past all relief,   i 271

At Polwart on the green,   i 273

A lass that was laden'd with care,   i 286

Alas, when charming Sylvia's gone,   i 295

At setting day and rising morn,   i 304

Auld Rob Morris that wins in yon glen,   ii 12

Although I be but a country lass,   ii 30

A southland Jenny that was right bonny,   ii 83

And I'll o'er the muir to Maggy,   ii 84

A cock-laird fou cadgie,   ii 35

A ladie and a lassie,   ii 87

As I sat at my spinning wheel,   ii 95

An I'll awa' to bonny Tweed-side,   ii 119

Alas, my son, you little know,   ii 120

As Jamie gay gang'd blyth his way,   ii 134
A friend of mine came here yeftreen,   ii 137
As I was walking ae May morning,   ii 165
As I came in by Fifherraw,   ii 181
As Patie came up frae the glen,   ii 188
And a' that e'er my Jenny had,   ii 204
As I came down bonny Tweed-fide,   ii 214
As I gaed to the well at e'en,   ii 220
And fare ye weel, my auld wife,   ii 222
As I walk'd by myfelf, I faid to myfelf,   ii 229
And there fhe's lean'd her back to a thorn,   ii 237

B

Balow, my boy, ly ftill and fleep,   i 65
Bufk ye, bufk ye, my bonny, bonny bride,   i 68
Beneath a green fhade a lovely young fwain,   i 193
Bufk ye, bufk ye, my bonny bride,   i 194
Beffy's beauties fhine fae bright,   i 196
By fmooth winding Tay a fwain was reclining,   i 227
Bleft as th' immortal gods is he,   i 235
Blyth Jocky young and gay,   i 235
Bright Cynthia's power divinely great,   i 241
By a murmuring ftream a fair fhepherdefs lay,   i 257
Beneath a green fhade I fand a fair maid,   i 262
By Pinky-houfe oft let me walk,   i 269
Beneath a beech's grateful fhade,   i 272
By the delicious warmnefs of thy mouth,   i 278
Beneath a green willow's fad ominous fhade,   ii 5
Blyth, blyth, blyth was fhe,   ii 18
But are you fure the news is true,   ii 152
Blyth young Befs to Jean did fay,   ii 154
Braw, braw lads of Galla-water,   ii 202
Bonny laffie, will ye go,   ii 221

C

Clavers and his Highlandmen,   i 102
Clerk Colvill and his lufty dame,   i 161
Care, away gae thou frae me,   ii 34
Come, carles a' of fumbler's ha',   ii 46
Come, let's hae mair wine in,   ii 94
Cauld be the rebel's caft,   ii 193
Cauld kale in Aberdeen,   ii 205

D

Dumbarton's drums beat bonny—O,   i 209
Duty and part of reason,   i 303
Deil tak the wars that hurried Billy from me,   i 306
Down in yon meadow a couple did tarry,   ii 38
Dear Roger, if your Jenny geck,   ii 191
Donald Cowper and his man,   ii 229

E

Earl Douglas, than quham nevir knicht,   i 144

F

Frae Dunidier as I came throuch,   i 37
From Spey to the border was peace and good order,   i 45
Falfe Sir John a-wooing came,   i 93
From anxious zeal and factious ftrife,   i 205
For ever, Fortune, wilt thou prove,   i 250
Farewel to Lochaber, and farewel my Jean,   i 236
For the lack of gold fhe's left me,   i 253
From Roflin caftle's echoing walls,   i 284
Falfe luve, and hae ze played me this,   ii 6
Fy let us a' to the bridal,   ii 24
For the fake of fomebody,   ii 41

G

Gil Morrice was an erle's fon,   i 1
God profper long our noble king,   i 54
Gilderoy was a bonny boy,   i 73
Good-morrow, fair miftrefs, the beginner of ftrife,   ii 5
Gin ye meet a bonny laffie,   ii 42
Gie me a lafs wi' a lump of land,   ii 66
Gude day now, bonny Robin,   ii 166
Gin I had a wee houfe and a canty wee fire,   ii 179
Gae to the ky wi' me, Johny,   ii 203
Gie my love brofe, brofe,   ii 203
Green grows the rafhes,   ii 224

H

How blythe ilk morn was I to fee,   i 181
Hear me, ye nymphs and every fwain,   i 190
How fweetly fmells the fimmer green,   i 198
How happy is the rural clown,   i 229
Happy's the love which meets return,   i 260

How can I be blyth or glad,   ii   1
Have you any pots or pans,   ii   32
Honeſt man, John Ochiltree,   ii   61
Hearken and I will tell you how,   ii   73
Here awa', there awa', here awa', Willie,   ii   140
How dan dilly dow,   ii   176
Herſel pe Highland ſhentleman,   ii   186
How ſhall I be ſad when a huſband I hae,   ii   193
Hid from himſelf, now by the dawn,   ii   194
Hey how, Johny lad, ye're no ſae kind's ye ſud
     hae been,   ii   215
How lang have I a batchelor been,   ii   218

I

It fell about the Martinmas,   i   8
It was in and about the Martinmas time,   i   19
It was on an evening ſae ſaft and ſae clear,   i   98
I've ſpent my time in rioting,   i   99
In the garb of old Gaul, wi' the fire of old Rome,   i   116
I weir'd, I weird, hard-hearted lord,   i   136
I dream'd a dreary dream laſt night,   i   145
It fell and about the Lammas-time,   i   153
I'll wager, I'll wager, I'll wager with you,   i   168
I've ſeen the ſmiling,   i   214
I will awa' wi' my love,   i   267
I had a heart, but now I heartleſs gae,   i   291
In April when primroſes paint the ſweet plain,   i   298
I yield, dear laſſie, ye have won,   i   300
In a garden ſae green, in a May morning,   i   308
In ancient times, as ſongs rehearſe,   i   310
I thought it ance a loneſome life,   ii   20
In yonder town there wons a May,   ii   23
In Scotland there liv'd a humble beggar,   ii   28
In January laſt,   ii   52
Jocky he came here to woo,   ii   55
Jocky fou, Jenny fain,   ii   59
I was ance a weel tocher'd laſs,   ii   63
Jocky met with Jenny fair,   ii   85
I hae a wee purſe, and a wee pickle gowd,   ii   94
In winter when the rain rain'd cauld,   ii   102

In Auchtermuchty dwelt a man, ii 125
I chanc'd to meet an airy blade, ii 132
I've been courting at a lafs, ii 135
I had a horfe, and I had nae mair, ii 151
It fell about the Martinmas time, ii 159
I rade to London yefterday, ii 163
I'll go to the green wood, ii 176
It was on a Sunday, ii 180
Jocky faid to Jenny, Jenny wilt thou do't, ii 195
John, come kifs me now, ii 206
I wifh that ye were dead, goodman, ii 207
I'll trip upon trenchers, I'll dance upon difhes, ii 231
I hae lain three herring a fa't, ii 225
I am a poor filly auld man, ii 224
In fimmer I mawed my meadows, ii 224

K

Keep ye weel frae Sir John Malcolm, ii 99
Keep the country, bonny laffie, ii 222

L

Lord Thomas and fair Annet, i 24
Lizie Wan fits at her father's bower-door, i 91
Little wat ye wha's coming, i 117
Liv'd ance twa lovers in yon dale, i 162
Love's goddefs in a myrtle grove, i 184
Leave kindred and friends, fweet Betty, i 196
Look where my dear Hamilla fmiles, i 197
Love never more fhall give me pain, i 263
Lizie Baillie's to Gartartane gane, ii 3
Late in an evening forth I went, ii 13
Laffie, lend me your braw hemp-heckle, ii 22
Look up to Pentland's tow'ring tops, ii 227
Logan water and Logan braes, ii 230

M

March, march, march, i 115
My fheep I neglected, I loft my fheep-hook, i 174
My Patie is a lover gay, i 206
My love was ance a bonny lad, i 216
My dear and only love, I pray, i 236

My dear and only love, take heed,   i 237
My foger-laddie is over the fea,   i 292
My Peggy is a young thing,   i 297
My love has built a bonny fhip and fet her on the fea,   ii   2
My Jockie blyth, for what thou'ft done,   ii 48
My daddy is a canker'd carl,   ii 64
Merry may the maid be,   ii 70
My fweeteft May, let love incline thee,   ii 99
My Jeanny and I have toil'd,   ii 107
My mither's ay glowran o'er me,   ii 118
My name is Argyle : you may think it ftrange,   ii 130
My daddy left me gear enough,   ii 143
My love was born in Aberdeen,   ii 179
My mither fent me to the well,   ii 208
My daddy he fteal'd the minifter's cow,   ii 221
My wife's a wanton wee thing,   ii 230

N

Now fpring begins her fmiling round,   i 185
No more my fong fhall be, ye fwains,   i 282
Now Phœbus advances on high,   i 287
Now from rufticity and love,   i 302
Nanfy's to the green-wood gane,   ii 79
Now wat ye wha I met yeftreen,   ii 117
Now the fun's gane out of fight,   ii 124

O

O liften, good people, to my tale,   i 21
Of all the Scottifh northern chiefs,   i 30
On July feventh, the futh to fay,   i 49
O waly, waly up the bank,   i 81
O wha will fhoe my bonny feet,   i 149
Oh, how could I venture to love ane like thee,   i 176
O Befly Bell and Mary Grey,   i 199
Once more I'll tune the vocal fhell,   i 202
On Whitfunday morning,   i 210
On Ettrick banks in a fummer's night,   i 212
O come awa' come awa',   i 225
O had awa', had awa',   i 226
O Bell, thy looks hae kill'd my heart,   i 228
One day I heard Mary fay,   i 233

O Mary, thy graces and glances,   i 285
O Sandy, why leaves thou thy Nelly to mourn,   i 294
O gin my love were yon red rofe,   ii   4
O my bonny, bonny May,   ii   6
O faw ye Jonnie cummin, quo' fhe,   ii 45
O Jeany, Jeany, where haft thou been,   ii 57
O mither dear, I 'gin to fear,   ii 58
O fteer her up and had her gawin,   ii 97
O wha's that at my chamber-door,   ii 111
O will you hae ta tartan plaid,   ii 160
O Johny Johnfton was my love,   ii 216
O leeze me on your curly pow,   ii 215
O luftie May, with Flora queen,   ii 212
O faw ye my father, or faw ye my mother,   ii 208
O have I burnt, or have I flain,   ii 202
Old King Coul was a jolly old foul,   ii 183
O laffie, art thou fleeping yet,   ii 167
Our gudeman came hame at e'en,   ii 172
O dear Peggy, love's beguiling,   ii 192
Our king he has a fecret to tell,   ii 231
O as I was kift yeftreen,   ii 226
O this is my departing time,   ii 225

P
Pain'd with her flighting Jamie's love,   i 258
Peggy, now the king's come,   ii 194

Q
Quhy dois zour brand fae drap wi' bluid,   i 63

R
Robin is my only jo,   i 311
Return hameward, my heart, again,   ii 43
Rob's Jock came to woo our Jenny,   ii 88

S
Sum fpeiks of lords, fum fpeiks of lairds,   i 13
Sound, found the mufic found it,   i 113
Stately ftept he eaft the wa',   i 119
Saw ye the thane of meikle pride,   i 131
She has called to her her bower-maidens,   i 148
She's prick'd herfel, and prin'd herfel,   i 159

A a 2

Should auld acquaintance be forgot, i 177
Stern winter has left us, the trees are in bloom, i 279
Saw ye nae my Peggy, i 288
Speak on, speak thus, and still my grief, i 299
Sweet Annie frae the sea-beach came, i 305
Some say kissing's a sin, ii 15
Saw ye Jenny Nettles, ii 60
Sweet sir, for your courtésie, ii 67
Somnolente quæso repénte, ii 98
Symon Brodie had a cow, ii 230

T

The king sits in Dumfermling toune, i 28
There came a ghost to Margaret's door, i 76
'Twas at the fearful midnight hour, i 78
There was three ladies in a ha', i 88
There's some say that we wan, i 104
The chevalier being void of fear, i 109
The rain runs down thro' Merry-land town, i 155
There gowans are gay, my joy, i 157
The knight stands in the stable door, i 165
The spring-time returns, and clothes the green plains, i 175
The smiling morn, the breathing spring, i 191
The collier has a daughter, i 207
The lawland lads think they are fine, i 222
The lawland maids gang trig and fine, i 224
Tho' for seven years and mair honour should reave me, i 232
'Tis not your beauty nor your wit, i 243
The last time I came o'er the moor, i 249
Tell me, Hamilla, tell me why, i 251
The morn was fair saft was the air, i 254
'Twas summer, and the day was fair, i 261
Tho' beauty, like the rose, i 274
The lass of Patie's mill, i 275
'Twas in that season of the year, i 283
The silent night her sables wore, i 289
The bonny grey-eyed morn begins to peep, i 305
'Twas early in the morning, a morning of May, ii 11
There was a wife wond in a glen, ii 16

There was a jolly beggar, and a begging he was bound,	ii	26
The carl he came o'er the craft,	ii	33
The pawkie auld carle came o'er the lee,	ii	49
The gypſies came to our good lord's gate,	ii	54
The maltman comes on Mananday,	ii	69
The meal was dear ſhort ſyne,	ii	76
'Tis I have ſeven braw new gowns,	ii	81
There was an auld wife had a wee pickle tow,	ii	92
Tarry woo, tarry woo,	ii	100
Tibby has a ſtore of charms,	ii	104
This is no mine ain houſe,	ii	105
There was ance a May, and ſhe lu'd na men,	ii	108
The widow can bake and the widow can brew,	ii	112
The yellow-hair'd laddie ſat down on yon brae,	ii	126
'Tis nae very lang ſinſyne,	ii	135
There was a bonny wee ladie,	ii	139
There liv'd a wife in our gate-end,	ii	140
The plowman he's a bonny lad,	ii	144
The tailor came to clout the claiſe,	ii	145
The maid's gane to the mill by night,	ii	148
There came a young man to my daddy's door,	ii	150
There was a ſhepherd's ſon,	ii	156
There's fouth of braw Jockies and Jennies,	ii	169
The ſhepherd's wife cries o'er the lee,	ii	182
There was a jolly miller once,	ii	185
The dorty will repent,	ii	192
The laird wha in riches and honour,	ii	194
'Twas at the ſhining mid-day hour,	ii	197
The mucking of Geordy's byre,	ii	201
The Wren ſhe lyes in care's bed,	ii	209
Tibby Fowler o' the glen,	ii	223
There gaed a fair maiden out to walk,	ii	226
There's a farmer near hard by,	ii	232
There dwells a tod on yonder craig,	ii	234
The prettieſt laird in a' the weſt,	ii	236
The country ſwain that haunts the plain,	ii	238

W

Willie's rare and Willie's fair,   i 85

When Frennet caftle's ivied wall,   i 142

Wha will bake my bridal bread,   i 167

Wert thou but mine ain thing,   i 173

When flow'ry meadows deck the year,   i 178

What numbers fhall the mufe repeat,   i 180

When fummer comes the fwains on Tweed,   i 182

When innocent paftime our pleafure did crown,   i 203

When trees did bud, and fields were green,   i 208

With tuneful pipe and hearty glee,   i 211

Will ye go to the ew-bughts, Marion,   i 213

Whoe'er beholds my Helen's face,   i 218

Why hangs that cloud upon thy brow,   i 231

When Jocky was bleft with your love and your
truth,   i 244

Whilft I alone your foul poffeft,   i 247

When Phœbus bright the azure fkies,   i 251

While fome for pleafure pawn their health,   i 264

What beauties does Flora difclofe,   i 293

With broken words and downcaft eyes,   i 295

When firft my dear laddie gaed to the green hill,   i 299

Were I affured you'll conftant prove,   i 301

Well, I agree, you're fure of me,   i 302

When hope was quite funk in defpair,   i 303

Wo worth the time and eke the place,   i 309

When Meggy and me were acquaint,   i 311

When I think on this warld's pelf,   ii 19

While fops in faft Italian verfe,   ii 37

When we come to London town,   ii 40

When I think on my lad, I figh and am fad,   ii 68

Wha wadna be in love,   ii 26

Whan I have a faxpence under my thumb,   ii 100

Where wad bonny Ann ly,   ii 113

Willie was a wanton wag,   ii 115

Woo'd and married and a',   ii 117

We're gayly yet, and we're gayly yet,   ii 121

When we went to the field of war,   ii 122

When the fheep are in the fauld, and the ky at hame,   ii 195

When firſt my dear Johny came to this town,   ii 205
When ſhe came ben ſhe bobbit,   ii 206
When I was a wee thing,   ii 213
Will ye go to the wood, quo' Fozie Mozie,   ii 210
Will ye go to Flanders, my Mally—O,   ii 223
When I gaed to the mill my lane,   ii 228
Where will we get a wife to you,   ii 235

Y

Ye Highlands and ye lawlands,   i 20
Ye ſylvan powers that rule the plain,   i 188
Ye gales that gently wave the ſea,   i 194
Ye gods, was Strephon's picture bleſt,   i 217
Ye watchful guardians of the fair,   i 221
Young Philander woo'd me lang,   i 276
You meaner beauties of the night,   i 281
Ye blytheſt lads and laſſes gay,   ii 63

THE END.

ADVERTISEMENT.

The Editor of the foregoing, propoſes to compile

A

COLLECTION

OF

SELECT ENGLISH SONGS.

IN TWO VOLUMES.